D0830834

70001704051 9

·O·O· CLEARLY

"Clearly performs an important service in bringing the issue of poor vision to the world's attention. The Clearly campaign, and this book, vividly shows us the cost, in human and economic terms, of so many of our fellow citizens being unable to see. New technology offers millions of the world's visually impaired ways to see and to turn text into audio. It is time for the world to act fast. If we fail to act, those left behind will never catch up."

GORDON BROWN, FORMER UK PRIME MINISTER

"With his Clearly campaign and this excellent book, James Chen has shone a light on an issue the world must now address. Too many of our fellow citizens suffer from poor vision for no other reason than they have never had access to an eye test and glasses. The cost in personal and economic terms is enormous. Good sight is the key to achieving many of our development goals. With his wonderful Vision for a Nation organisation in Rwanda, in cooperation with the Ministry of Health, James has shown a visionary way forward. Governments across the developing world should follow their example. This is an important book. Health and economic ministers everywhere no longer have an excuse for ignoring the problem of correctable poor vision."

ANDREW MITCHELL, FORMER UK SECRETARY OF STATE FOR INTERNATIONAL DEVELOPMENT

"I admire James Chen's mission to help the billions of people on our planet with poor vision. In a world where we have made unprecedented progress, it is unforgivable that so many still struggle to see clearly. The time for the whole world to see has come."

HELLE THORNING-SCHMIDT, CEO OF SAVE THE CHILDREN INTERNATIONAL, FORMER PRIME MINISTER OF DENMARK

"James Chen is living proof that often the greatest progress for humanity can come from personal setback for one human being. From a failed eye test when he applied for a driving permit was born Chen's lifelong obsession to help the whole world see.

With 2.5 billion people unable to see properly, and unable to get basic eye care, Chen and his Clearly campaign are leaders in highlighting the greatest unmet disability of our times. They have shown, in Rwanda, how this problem can be fixed. And now he is determined to fix it for the world. This is a compelling story, well told, of that rare thing in the world – someone with a really bold vision who has the resources, the determination and the inspiration to make it happen."

ALASTAIR CAMPBELL, WRITER, COMMUNICATOR AND STRATEGIST, FORMER BRITISH PRIME MINISTER TONY BLAIR'S DIRECTOR OF COMMUNICATIONS

"James Chen has dedicated his life's work to ensuring that everyone has access to basic eye care. Poor vision affects 2.5 billion people. Despite readily available solutions, access to basic eye care remains a barrier, leaving many unable to see properly.

Chen and his Clearly campaign recognise that health is a human right and have addressed the problem of poor vision in Rwanda by supporting the Ministry of Health to integrate eye care in the primary health system. Together, we have shown that good eye care does not just improve general wellness, but also has a fantastic economic return for individuals, families, local communities, and the entire country.

Chen's new mission is to improve eye-care services for the entire world. This is the compelling story of how one man with a bold vision and an unwavering passion invested his resources to make his dreams a reality."

PROFESSOR AGNES BINAGWAHO, VICE-CHANCELLOR, UNIVERSITY OF GLOBAL HEALTH EQUITY, FORMER MINISTER OF HEALTH, RWANDA

"As a lifetime wearer of specs, I was shocked to learn that a third of the world's population cannot see properly purely because they have never had access to an eye test and the glasses they need to go about their daily lives. As James rightly says, it is unacceptable and it is a scandal that the world must address. The economics are a no-brainer. Helping people see will increase the world's productivity and boost the learning of young people.

More important than that, it will make a huge difference to the quality of life of the 2.5 billion people who just need a pair of glasses. This book is a wake-up call. I hope it inspires the people who have the power to make things right to do just that.

James Chen is a true visionary whose Clearly campaign and this totally excellent book has done an enormous service to the world."

KEVIN CAHILL CBE, FORMER CEO AND HONORARY LIFE PRESIDENT OF COMIC RELIEF

"In *Clearly*, philanthropist James Chen highlights a global problem too long neglected: the 2.5 billion people worldwide who cannot see clearly, but for whom a simple pair of glasses is beyond their reach. With one-third of the global population affected, poor vision may be the largest unaddressed disability in the world today.

Poor vision is a barrier to progress on so many levels, hindering education, employment opportunities and productivity. Chen presents the barriers people face in the developing world to acquiring glasses – a 700-year-old invention – as well as ready solutions to eliminate these barriers. It is a must-read for any policy maker who is serious about education, poverty reduction, closing the equity gap and achieving the 2030 development goals. In health costs and lost productivity alone, poor vision carries a global cost of trillions of dollars per year.

This book is just what we need to kickstart action and drive the change needed – to work together so no one is left behind for lack of a pair of glasses."

JUSTIN FORSYTH, DEPUTY EXECUTIVE DIRECTOR UNICEF

"I am excited to endorse this book both in my role as CEO of Sightsavers and personally as someone whose extreme short-sightedness was discovered at a school screening programme when I was six. Sightsavers is dedicated to fighting avoidable visual impairment in developing countries, whether that be through strengthening eye health systems or ensuring people are able to access eye tests and spectacles. The issue has not had the attention it deserves – poor eyesight makes it more difficult to get a good education, hampers job opportunities and therefore damages economies. It also means people miss out on beautiful sights – a sunrise, their grandchildren – things beyond price. So I welcome James Chen's involvement wholeheartedly."

CAROLINE HARPER, CEO OF SIGHTSAVERS

"Right now, life as we know it is being disrupted by a technological revolution. Yet 2.5 billion people are being left out of benefiting from progress because they lack something so basic – a pair of glasses.

Through his work with Clearly, James Chen reveals the mind-boggling problem of a world where inventions from drones and 3D printing to virtual reality are becoming commonplace, but we haven't found a way to put a pair of glasses on the noses of everyone with poor eyesight.

His mission to bring pioneering entrepreneurs and new technology together, to mobilise this old invention for the good of everyone, is as uplifting as it is innovative. A true visionary."

RUSS SHAW, FOUNDER OF GLOBAL TECH ADVOCATES AND TECH LONDON ADVOCATES

HOW A 700 YEAR OLD INVENTION CAN CHANGE THE WORLD FOREVER

·O·O·
CLEARLY

JAMES CHEN

Biteback Publishing

First published in Great Britain in 2017 by
Biteback Publishing Ltd
Westminster Tower
3 Albert Embankment
London SE1 7SP
Copyright © James Chen 2017

ISBN 978-1-78590-270-3

10 9 8 7 6 5 4 3 2 1

A CIP catalogue record for this book is available from the British Library.

Set in Lyon Text

Printed and bound in Great Britain by
CPI Group (UK) Ltd, Croydon CR0 4YY

This book is dedicated to my late father, Robert Yet-Sen Chen,
who, despite having to overcome much hardship in his life,
inspired so many with his kindness, decency and determination
to leave the world better than when he arrived.

ACKNOWLEDGEMENTS

I have made it my life's work to help the world to see, but it all started with an interesting investment idea with a social mission: Adlens' adjustable power lenses for glasses. This evolved into a journey of enlightenment in Vision for a Nation's Rwanda initiative, tackling the challenges and invisible barriers around the issue of access to vision correction in the developing world. The brilliant TED Talk by Dr Andrew Bastawrous about his smartphone app Peek Vision, coupled with our learnings from Rwanda, sparked my most recent and most ambitious campaign – Clearly.

Andrew has since become a friend and, as I reflect on my incredible journey to date, what stands out is the thought that without the goodwill and support of colleagues and compatriots like Andrew, of whom there have been so many, my journey would have been so much more difficult, if not impossible. I feel lucky and blessed to have benefited from their trust, expertise and friendship.

Over the past thirteen years, so many colleagues have contributed to bringing the adjustable power lens technologies to the benefit of the public at Adlens and Adaptive Eyewear. The brilliant and always disruptive Professor Josh Silver, forever with a cheeky twinkle in his eyes. The equally brilliant Dr Rob Stevens, our long serving Chief Technology Officer. Dr Graeme MacKenzie, a research optometrist by training, exceptionally knowledgeable, multi-talented and my long-est-serving colleague, to whom I turn when I am lost. My dear friend, shareholder and board member Hamilton Tang. Board members past and present: Dean Butler, Dave Chute, Remi Corlin, Greg Nugent, Mike Nuttall and Dame Sue Street. CEOs Sjoerd Hannema, Mike Ferrara, John Kennedy and Julian Lambert, who recently lost his battle with cancer. Julian, with a distinguished career in the development sector, took a secondment from the Department for International Development to lead Adaptive Eyewear in an ill-fated attempt to persuade the World Bank to support the deployment of adjustable power glasses in the developing world, and I credit him with recommending that we focus our efforts on Rwanda in what would become Vision for a Nation (VFAN).

Dr Agnes Binagwaho as Permanent Secretary of the Rwandan Ministry of Health immediately understood the potential impact of Vision for a Nation's proposed project in Rwanda and she took a chance on this brand new organisation with no record of accomplishment to team up with the Ministry of Health to establish primary eye care in Rwanda. She continued to be our champion as Minister of Health and described our partnership as a model public–private partnership. If not for her taking a risk on the upstart VFAN and her unwavering support, we could not have accomplished as much in Rwanda and in the timescale to complete the mission. John Rhodes, as chairman of the board of trustees, has ably led us through thick and thin along with fellow trustees Catherine Colloms, Arnold Ekpe, Alex Scott, Paul Tomasic and I. As CEO, Tom Rosewall applied his deep business management experience, took a faltering effort in Rwanda, and transformed the operations into a focused, results-oriented machine, with Tony Hulton now developing plans to take VFAN beyond Rwanda. Abdallah Uwihoreye, our ever-resourceful Rwanda country director and our trusted eyes and ears on the ground with his team, John Asiimwe, Bizimungu Emile, Clarisse Dusabimana, Innocent Habimana, Reuben Kalisa, Agnes Safari Mbabazi, Joseph Munana, Chance Pascal, Evode Rwasamanzi, Sarah Day Smith, Pascal Umugwaneza, Charlotte Umurerwa, Cyriaca Uwababyeyi, Pacifique Uwamahoro and Marie Ange Uwase. Dr Ciku Mathenge, who created the eye test protocol used so successfully in Rwanda and Dr John Nkurikiye, who built the support of the professional eye community and within the government. UK team members Peter Desmond, Sebastian Ford and Sebastian Ling.

Greg Nugent, who also serves as a director of Adlens, is my partner in Clearly and the wizardly mastermind behind this campaign. The 'first follower' to build this movement, to whom I am eternally grateful, he has mobilised his entire company, Inc. London, along with his business partner Godric Smith to drive this campaign forward as the firm's commitment to social impact. Thank you, Inc. London. Compatriots of the Clearly team seconded from Inc. London include the most able Will Straw, who I hope one day will lead Britain onto the right path, the meticulous Phil Webster, who has put my story into this book, Marion Allene, Charleen Cannone, Simon Darvill, Julie Fenton, Nina Ferrier, Morgan George, Katie Heywood, Jo Irwin, Nicola Minford, Neil Minott, Alex Oates, Kate Potts, Jemma Thompson and Charlotte Todman. The trustees of Clearly Initiatives: Penny Chu, Nick Mercer and Paul Tomasic. At Seven Hills, the mission-driven PR and communications firm, co-founders Nick Giles and Michael

Hayman have dedicated resources to this campaign beyond the call of duty, Charlotte Hastings, who makes me look smart, at least in front of the media, Matic Boh, Becky Emery, Henny Hamilton, Rachel Ringstead and Hannah Sewell.

Jennifer Chen, Phoebe Ma, Gladys Choy and Linda Tsui, colleagues at my family office Legacy Advisors, ably dealing with the myriad details allowing me the freedom to do what I do best.

Many sector and domain experts contributed their knowledge and expertise openly to the writing of this book, including Peter Ackland, Astrid Bonfield, Brian Doolan, Kristan Gross, Caroline Harper, Jordan Kassalow, Jonathan Ledgard, Will Hetzler, William Mapham, Jacob Mohan, Kovin Naidoo, Ollie Rickman, J. C. Hinsley, Michael Conway, Rupert Ellwood, Natalie Au, Lucy Hopkins-Parkinson and Liz Smith. My friends Vikram Gandhi, Steve Greer, Gwen Rehnborg and Araminta Whitley took the time to plough through early drafts of this book and provided invaluable feedback.

This book is dedicated to my late father Robert, but it is the support of my entire family that has given me the strength and the resources to pursue and persevere in this wondrously challenging journey of discovery and purpose. My mother Daisy, so intuitive and resolute, the bedrock of our family. My wife Su, whose patience and love for a card-carrying member of the 'league of misfits and outliers' keeps me grounded. Our kids, Jack, Jamie and Jake, have grown up experiencing my struggles and personal challenges to live up to the saying 'to whom much is given, of whom much is expected'. Finally, my dear sister Margaret, who passed away in 2016, at the age of fifty-two after a long struggle with her personal demons, tragic and heartbreaking and a great loss to our family.

CONTENTS

PART I

THE SCANDAL THE WORLD FORGOT

CHAPTER 1

WAKE UP WORLD

More than 700 years ago, spectacles were invented. One of the greatest innovations in our history had arrived.

In those early years, perhaps only aristocrats and the clergy experienced the joy of reading. But the invention of the Gutenberg press in around 1440 meant that very quickly there was a mass audience wanting to read, and requiring glasses if they could not see properly. Over the centuries, as aesthetics improved and our understanding of the eye advanced, we have become so comfortable wearing glasses that we now buy them in all sorts of shapes and sizes. Would Steve Jobs or Bill Gates have been able to code without their glasses? How would Elton John have learned the piano? Would the magical world of Harry Potter ever have been created if J. K. Rowling didn't have a pair of specs?

This book is about the unfulfilled potential of getting this centuries-old innovation on the noses of all the people who need it. Despite the fact that so many of us wear the latest Tom Ford glasses, still, to this day, a staggering 2.5 billion people who need a pair of glasses don't have them.[1] In many instances, they simply cannot get hold of a pair because local markets for affordable glasses do not exist. Or, sadly, they do not understand the simple and proven benefits of spectacles.

Framed negatively, this is an oversight of epic and historical proportions. How did we miss this? How did we skip something so simple and so beneficial to humanity? Although I am tempted to take this path, I am also reluctant, as I am optimistic about the power of public policy, markets and people to change the world. So instead I will try to frame this positively.

Sight is the golden thread of human development. We have a proven, tested, legal and highly desirable product that can change billions of lives in an instant. The romantic in me wants to make that case in this book. But to make that argument I need to start with the facts, as they are alarming and they make me want to shout out, loudly, 'Wake up world'.

Today, an estimated 2.5 billion people, just under the combined population of China and India, cannot see clearly and yet have no access to a sight test and a simple pair of glasses.

In a world of huge opportunities for those who can see clearly, we have a third of the planet's population who are being held back by the biggest oversight in history.

Poor vision is the largest unaddressed disability in the world today, but for decades it has been at best forgotten and at worst ignored. Governments, the United Nations, the World Health Organization (WHO) – none have done enough to acknowledge this problem and act on it.

Helping the world to see is about so much more than health. It's about the future of our children, because a child who cannot see a blackboard cannot get a decent education; it's about gender equality, because far more women suffer than men; and it's about productivity, because if you cannot see clearly, it's difficult or impossible to work. Not least, it is about the mental health and dignity of the individual to feel stimulated, productive and self-sufficient.

The time for action is now, because the phenomenal technological change taking place in the world looks set to leave behind anyone who cannot participate in progress. By 2020, most people in the world will have access to a smartphone. In the next five years, another three billion consumers will come online. 3D printers will transform production costs. More and more people will spend their working lives at computers. We must ensure that no one is left behind because they cannot see clearly.

We have a chance now to correct this. It is critical that governments, global authorities, non-governmental organisations (NGOs), and the public at large understand the scale of this problem and work together to solve it. That is why I set up the Clearly campaign – to draw the world's attention to this scandal and to start a debate about how we solve it.

It will cost money, but the investment will be repaid so many times over that I believe the economists and finance ministries will not struggle with the 'business case'.

Poor vision is costing us all trillions of dollars a year in health costs and lost productivity.[2] Imagine the huge benefits if all those people without proper sight could use computers, read books or carry out mechanical tasks that poor vision prevents them from doing today.

And, unlike many other development challenges facing the world, there is a solution, and it comes from the old world – glasses!

A recent survey in the *Atlantic* magazine to assess the top fifty innovations that had shaped modern life put optical lenses at number five.[3] The author, James Fallows, wrote that the adoption of corrective lenses 'amounted to the largest onetime IQ boost in human history' – a startling statement that graphically illustrates the inequity and iniquity of the fact that, centuries after the arrival of spectacles, so many in the world don't have access to them.

And we are hardly touching this problem. As Jordan Kassalow, founder of VisionSpring, a social enterprise that is one of the leaders in this field, tells us later in this book, his organisation has distributed over 4 million pairs of glasses over the past fifteen years in some developing countries. 'But as we did that it has become more and more apparent that if that figure was 10 million or 100 million we would still only be making a dent in this worldwide problem.'

A step change is needed if we are to make glasses and other treatments available to everyone who needs them. The visionaries of old, the people who gave us spectacles, must have their work completed by the visionaries of today.

But there are four big barriers to achieving this – what I call the four Ds: diagnosis, distribution, dollars and demand.

First, there are simply not enough people carrying out the relatively simple task of diagnosing someone's eyesight. State regulations mean that in many countries screening people to see whether they are short- or far-sighted can only be done by eye doctors with years of training. But only a tiny proportion of these experts live in the developing world. We must train thousands more people – from community nurses to teachers to entrepreneurs – to carry out basic sight tests. This would also free up the eye professionals to focus on more serious eye diseases which only they are qualified to address.

Second, we must distribute glasses to those who need them. If we can get a bottle of cola to villages across the world, surely we can deliver a pair of glasses? Yet rules and regulations in many countries stop local shops or kiosks from selling reading glasses, and only a handful of countries have been brave enough to take on the eye health industry and allow prescription glasses to be sold over the counter. As a result, millions of people – including children at the start of their lives – are denied a simple solution to their vision problem.

Third, we must cut the cost of glasses by ensuring they can retail at dollars rather tens of dollars. A lengthy and complicated supply chain means that by the time glasses reach their users, several people have taken their 'cut' and unnecessarily hiked the final cost. There is no true free market in glasses anywhere in the world. Many governments exacerbate this problem by imposing heavy import duties and taxes on glasses, which render them unaffordable for most consumers in the developing world. Whereas imposing these taxes and duties on fashion-branded eyewear is understandable, non-branded eyewear should be exempt and viewed for what it is: an economic tool to boost productivity.

And fourth, the stigma over wearing glasses persists in the developing world, meaning that there is insufficient demand. Glasses are still not seen as a necessity; indeed, to some they imply a sense of weakness. Cultural barriers in some countries mean that women in particular are deterred from wearing them. We need to understand and overcome these obstacles if we are to succeed. Fixing the supply side is simply not enough.

Fortunately, overcoming these barriers is at the forefront of many of the brightest minds in the world.

My entry into the field of eye care was inspired by innovation. I had a chance encounter with Professor Josh Silver, the man who first saw the full potential of the modern fluid-filled adjustable lens, which allows the user to adjust their glasses to see clearly at any distance. I immediately grasped the potential of these lenses in the developing world, where distribution and logistics are fragile and expensive.

I had already begun to wonder whether my family's philanthropic foundation could do more to make an international impact, going beyond what was until then more geographically focused work in Asia. Because of my encounter with Josh, my eyewear company Adlens was founded.

We then considered how we could help the developing world with this groundbreaking advance. We considered several African countries, including Ghana, Ethiopia, Kenya and Rwanda, as possible candidates. Rwanda was chosen because of the relatively small size of the population and the relative ease of reaching every part of the country from its capital, Kigali. Rwanda is far from perfect, but its government has developed a burgeoning reputation for competence and good governance after the horrors of the past. As a result, Vision for a Nation, a charity committed to delivering eye care and affordable glasses for all, was born.

Rwanda is a trailblazer, becoming the first developing country in the world to provide access to vision screenings and affordable glasses to anyone who needs them. It has embraced self-adjustable glasses and has eased its rules to allow 2,500 community nurses to be trained in just three days to carry out sight tests and diagnose patients rather than attending a four-year university-level degree course in optometry. Meanwhile, Rwanda has deregulated the sale of eyewear so they are available throughout the country and not just in opticians, removed cost-increasing taxes and import duties on glasses, and developed an outreach programme in 15,000 villages to break down cultural barriers.

We need that kind of deregulation at different levels of the industry, and across Asia, Africa and Latin America, if we are to crack the problem of poor vision once and for all. With the will, this extraordinary achievement could be rolled out across the globe.

A lightbulb moment for me came when I saw a TED Talk from Dr Andrew Bastawrous showing how a smartphone could take a relatively high-resolution picture of the retina using hardware he had developed. I felt immediately that if a mobile could capture a good enough retinal image for diagnosis with minimal training, it could be one of the keys to universal access.

We need that technology and apps like Vula Mobile, the winner of my $250,000 Clearly Vision Prize, which connects healthcare workers in remote locations who have carried out vision screenings with eye specialists who are primarily based in urban areas.

In this book, I will tell their stories, reflect on their insights and look to the future too. Will we be able to use drones to drop supplies of glasses to distant places? What role could 3D printers play in crashing the cost of glasses? How close are we to developing eyedrops that correct vision through nanotechnology rather than spectacles? How can we encourage local designers and entrepreneurs to create affordable but attractive frames to break down the stigma of wearing glasses? What is the role for artificial intelligence?

As we have seen, spectacles were not popularised until the fifteenth century. We may be on the verge of something similar today as new technologies heighten the demand for vision correction.

But the task of helping the whole world see cannot be left to inventors and entrepreneurs alone. It must now dominate the thinking of global authorities everywhere.

What little money is available from governments and NGOs is primarily channelled to treating avoidable blindness. Around 165 million people have severe problems like cataracts, glaucoma and trachoma which need specialist treatment and maybe operations. They are and should be the priority.

But the number facing preventable blindness represents less than 10 per cent of those with poor vision. Little money is spent on the 2.5 billion people who may need only a vision screening and a pair of glasses to see clearly.

Access to vision correction is so low on development priorities that it did not feature in the sustainable development goals set by the United Nations in 2015. It is hard to imagine several of these objectives being achieved without people being able to see clearly. Simply put, clear vision is the 'golden thread' that runs through development, helping to achieve global goals on good health, quality education, decent work, gender equality and – of course – poverty elimination.

Despite the myopia of some international organisations, progress is being made in some of the most unlikely parts of the world. This book documents the amazing work of organisations like Sightsavers and the Fred Hollows Foundation which work tirelessly to tackle vision in the developing world.

Now global authorities need to take notice. The next Commonwealth summit will be in London in the spring of 2018. Of the 2.35 billion Commonwealth citizens, 1.2 billion – just over half – need glasses, but 900 million of those cannot get them.

The last summit in 2015 committed to tackling preventable blindness, so the Commonwealth has promising form on this issue. Extending the agenda to cover the goal of clear vision for all would seem logical. We hope the communiqué emerging from the summit will commit to unlocking the full potential of sight as quickly as possible by increasing access to affordable glasses throughout the Commonwealth.

If humans are to be on Mars by the 2030s, or even earlier, as many predict, it will be to the world's shame if everyone cannot see it happen.

The World Health Organization has estimated it could cost $28 billion over five years to tackle poor vision caused by refractive error.[4] Over ten years, the additional investment required to eliminate avoidable blindness in the developing world is estimated to be $128.2 billion.[5]

But just $850 million is spent by the top ten eye-care NGOs each year – primarily on tackling avoidable blindness.[6]

Entrepreneurs are doing their bit to bring down the cost. But we also need governments to step up. We must convince world governments that universal eye care is ultimately self-financing. If donors are looking for results, the answer is in eye care.

-O-O-

If you are reading this, there's a one in two chance that you're doing so with a pair of glasses or contact lenses. Just imagine what your life would be like without them.

I failed an eye test when I was just fifteen after applying for a driving permit. We were living in upstate New York at the time. It was a blow to my self-esteem, but not a lasting one. I got my first pair of glasses and, wow, the world I had lived in for fifteen years suddenly became clearer.

Now I knew what I had been missing. There would never, ever, be any chance of going back to a world without glasses. Life was better and I was more assured of the world around me. I was fortunate. So many are not.

I spent much of my early life in Nigeria. I remember how few Africans were wearing glasses, whereas many expatriates from richer countries were.

That memory is what inspires me. It cannot be right that clear vision is a lottery when the technology is so old and the costs are increasingly affordable. That's why I'm devoting my life to helping the whole world see, and I want to inspire you to sign up to my mission.

In this book, I will write about the eye, how it works and the invention of corrective lenses. I describe the work of the giants in this field and the inventions that will help us on our way. I write about the huge cost of this problem and tell the stories of people whose lives have been changed in Rwanda and elsewhere by the provision of glasses.

As you'll find, I'm not fatalistic. I believe that with the right political will, we can tackle the world's most intractable problems. But the issue of poor vision has been forgotten. So we are going to have to make a lot of noise. We also need to be practical, which is why I will use this book to set out my blueprint for how we tackle this issue.

Blueprint

Diagnosis:

1) Empowering practitioners: Restrictions preventing health workers, nurses or teachers from carrying out straightforward tasks like vision screening should be swept away.

2) Simpler diagnosis: The use of smartphones to screen vision must spread across the developing world rather than being confined to certain countries and age groups.

Distribution:

3) Market creation: Governments and NGOs must pump-prime or subsidise the provision of glasses to the poorest people in developing countries to help the eventual development of an open market. Global authorities like the United Nations and Commonwealth must wake up to this problem and recognise explicitly that global prosperity cannot be achieved without clear vision for all.

4) Removing inappropriate regulations: Restrictions on selling glasses over the counter should be removed so that shops around the world can stock glasses alongside other items such as biscuits and soft drinks.

5) Simpler supply chains: Entrepreneurs must be allowed to import glasses, transport them, screen people's eyesight and provide them with glasses, drastically simplifying the expensive supply chain.

Dollars:

6) Cutting costs: Governments must eliminate import duties and taxes on non-fashion glasses.

7) Unlocking technology: All exciting technological developments – for example the 3D printing of glasses, the use of drones for delivery, and artificial intelligence to detect eye disease – must be studied to see how they can help us achieve our aims.

Demand:

8) Eliminating cultural barriers: We must sensitively use role models and cultural figures to break down taboos over wearing glasses.

-O-O-

We cannot escape the fact that 700 years after glasses were invented the world has been prepared to tolerate a situation where billions of people still cannot see clearly.

New inventions mean that vision screenings and glasses have never been more affordable. But the pace of technological change means that if we don't act quickly we will condemn a third of the world's population to miss out on this progress.

On the flip side, if we get this right – ensuring that states and markets work together so that everyone has access to a sight test and an affordable pair of glasses – we will achieve a radical leap in productivity, prosperity and opportunity. This will be of benefit, yes, to those 2.5 billion people and the many more yet to be born who have poor vision. But it will also be to the good of everyone who can already see clearly, by creating more human ingenuity, more human creativity and more human happiness.

No longer can we let down the forgotten billions. It's time to wake up and help the whole world see.

CHAPTER 2

GLASSES CHANGE LIVES

Augustin Ngarambe pushed himself up from a chair and shuffled with the help of a large walking stick towards the nurse about to screen his eyes near a village in the eastern province of Rwanda.

Out in the open air but shaded by the beautiful trees in this 'outreach' called Zinga were around twenty people who had walked, some of them many miles, to have their eyes tested by Bosco Maniragena, a nurse trained to do the task under a scheme organised by Vision for a Nation (VFAN).

Bosco had spent the morning at Munyaga health centre a few miles away and then come down to the village of Rwisange to conduct the eye examinations at the outreach. By mid-afternoon, when the Clearly team arrived on a research visit, many local residents had already been screened and begun their walks home. Rwanda's main roads are good but Munyaga lies at the end of an eight-mile bumpy dirt track off one of the routes heading east. As happened throughout the visit, young children on the side of the road waved and shouted as the team passed.

Now it was Augustin's turn and he looked apprehensive as Bosco sat him down in a chair about four metres away from an eye chart. Covering one eye at a time, he was asked to read the letters on the chart to test his distance vision, and later he was given a similar chart to hold about two feet away from his eyes to test his near vision. The nurse then shone a light and looked into Augustin's eyes. After further consultations with an ophthalmic clinical officer, Nyiraneza Veneranda, who had come to the village with the Clearly observers, Bosco decided that Augustin should be referred to Rwamagana Hospital several miles away for further tests.

Augustin was one of some 200,000 people who have been referred for further testing by health centres and village outreaches under the VFAN programme since the end of 2012. That is about 10 per cent of the total screenings, which, remarkably, passed the 2 million mark in July 2017, well ahead of target. Some 150,000 reading and distance glasses had been prescribed and dispensed by that time and over a million people had been given eye drops to deal with infections. Those figures show just how much can be achieved if bodies like VFAN can cooperate with the national government to make it happen. By the end of 2017, it was hoped that all 15,000 villages in Rwanda would have been screened. It is a hugely ambitious project but I am delighted to say we are well on the way to achieving it.

On that visit, and on another the next day to an outreach in the southern province, the Clearly visitors saw many happy customers, their faces wreathed in smiles after they put on glasses for the first time and realised that whatever vision problems they had could be simply cured.

At that point, if they had 1,000 Rwandan francs (about £1) on their person, they could hand it over and get their life-changing new possession. If they did not have the money, they were given a prescription note and would take it to the nearest health centre as soon as they could pay for the glasses. Sadly, as we found, far too many people still do not go ahead and purchase the glasses after being prescribed them. Some have issues with the aesthetics; others decide after trying them on that they do not need them for their daily lives or have other, more pressing uses for their disposable income. Still others may feel self-conscious or fear ridicule.

But let us get back to our friend Augustin, now seventy, who had a moving story to tell us.

Augustin had been a successful builder in Kigali and, by Rwandan standards, led a reasonably comfortable life, able to put some of his six children through high school. But about twenty years ago he started getting dizzy spells when he was working. He was treated for high blood pressure but his sight problems persisted and he decided to move to the countryside to do what millions of Rwandans do – farm.

'I was a constructor. I could no longer do it because I would get dizzy. I could go up and fall down. But now I cultivate slowly, slowly because of not seeing well. And when the sun shines I go back home,' he said.

As he spoke, a plane flew overhead, a reminder of the modern world in this village so far removed from it.

'I used to be able to see a plane like that,' he said, pointing upwards. 'But then I saw two planes instead of one. And when the evening came I could not see at all. When it is dark someone might be there and I would not know who it was, until I talked to them.'

With his savings, he said in his native Kinyarwanda, he was able to buy five cows, but as his income has fallen through the years he has had to sell four of them to pay the school fees. 'When I arrived here I was still strong and I started constructing some of these houses here. But then I had to stop. All I could do was pray.'

Four of his children are still studying, two at high school and two at university. But even one of those who graduated still has no job.

He heard from a friend that the nurses were coming to the village and slowly walked several miles to get to the outreach.

His examination and the reassuring words of Bosco had given him hope that the hospital might be able to treat his condition, and he was glad that he had made the journey, rendered even more difficult because of his bad leg. 'Until today I thought I might die blind. I was feeling hopeless. Now I have hope because the hospital may be able to help me,' he told us.

Augustin's case is a heart-rending example of exactly why I have launched this campaign to give everyone a chance to see. His case is important to us for a key reason. VFAN is the only NGO in Rwanda dedicated to primary eye care, but the high number of referrals from health centres and village outreaches show that we are performing an important service that should lighten the load on secondary and tertiary eye care, whether by government or NGOs. It should show NGOs focused on secondary care – cataracts and the like – that VFAN can save them money and allow them to focus their expertise on what they do best.

And they do need convincing. For too many NGOs, primary eye care is still the work of optometrists who have gone through years of training.

With our revolutionary programme, VFAN, working with the Ministry of Health, has trained more than 2,500 nurses to carry out screening under our special three-day course.

Later in the book, I will explain further how the story of VFAN began, how it operates and what will happen next.

But let me first tell you about others whom the Clearly team saw being helped.

The day after the Zinga outreach, the Clearly visitors met up with Sam Ndihakaniye, who had been tested and prescribed with the adjustable glasses that were an early part of my journey and that of VFAN, although they make up only 9 per cent of the glasses distributed in the country under our scheme.

They went to the Muyumbu health centre in the Rwamagana district and were introduced to Sam, a delightful man who sang the praises of the glasses he had been given a few weeks earlier, talking of how they had changed the way he looked at life.

They gave him a lift from the centre to his home several miles away and he eagerly joined friends and relatives to do a bit of cultivating on their cooperative farm.

Then, outside his house a few yards away, Sam told of his life. Between 1986 and 2007, he served in the Rwandan Army, a period that covered the genocide years. He trained as an electrician in the army and was not involved in armed combat, installing electrical wiring in military properties.

On retiring from the army, he came back to the farm to work. He has a wife and three children, one very young. Two years ago, he found that his eyes were letting him down. His distance vision was troubling him and he was also getting headaches when reading.

Everything was blurry and as it became dark in the evenings he found it very hard to see anything. It meant he had trouble doing normal farm tasks.

Reading was becoming problematic. I would experience headaches. I would feel tears and think that maybe something was stuck in my eyes. I felt hopeless because I felt that my eyes were going to fail me completely. I would be blind. I thought that in a short while I would need to be guided as I walked. I was starting to give up, worrying whether I was going to go completely blind. I felt like life was going to stop.

He feared that he would never have enough money to pay for glasses or treatment.

Then, just recently, he heard on the radio a message that he could go for an eye examination at a local health centre and he decided to go. He made the long walk and was prescribed with his glasses and given some eye drops to help an infection. He says:

My life is normal again. I have got control again. I had the 1,000 francs and it has done so much for my life. The hopelessness has gone. I am happy. I feared I would die blind but now I know that I just needed these glasses. I can read with the children but I can also see what I am doing. Without good vision, life is so difficult. It is something everyone should have.

He added: 'Good vision is essential because when you can't see there is nothing you can achieve – life seems over. My work can now continue without any hindrance.'

The Clearly team's mission was not over and the story I am about to tell you shows all the reasons why I am determined to help crack this problem.

They drove back to Kigali and headed an hour's drive south towards another outreach. Again, it was miles from the main road and the track they used to get there would have been impassable for most vehicles. The outreach was called Kigusa; it was in Rugarama village and was served by Nyagihamba health centre.

It was very late in the day when they finally arrived but there was still a queue of people to see the nurse, and the examination room was surrounded by scores of lovely young children curious about the arrival of the *mzungu*. As everywhere, they shouted *muraho* (hi!) and high-fived the Clearly team whenever they got the chance.

During the day, the outreach nurses saw eighty-three people and prescribed twenty-two pairs of glasses.

It was here that the Clearly travellers were delighted to meet Maria Nyiranzayire. They watched as she had her near and far eye test, which resulted in her getting adjustable glasses.

Maria lost her husband in 1991 when the genocide had its first stirrings and was left to bring up her two boys on her own. Her younger son Rukundo was only four months old when his father died; he is now twenty-five but lives away from the village. They were very poor as a family without her husband and worked on a farm where they grew various crops. The children went to primary school but they did not go on to study later.

'We used to grow cassava [a root vegetable],' Maria says, 'but the seasons have been bad and it is four years since we grew them. I grow beans, sweet potatoes, soya, maize and tomatoes.'

Her vision problems began in 2000 and have never improved. She went to a health centre in Kabgayi and was given eyedrops. They dealt with the problem at the time but as she got older the problem got worse and she found she could not sort beans.

I just found that normal activities at home were becoming more and more difficult to do. When I am sick, I don't sleep. I wished I had sleeping pills but never got them. I feared I might end up being blind. I wondered what would happen if I became completely blind.

At one stage she went to a hospital to be checked, but without success. Then she heard the nurses were coming to the village on this very day and came along in the hope they might be able to do something.

I came here today because I heard they were going to do an eye assessment for all people. I thought it might help me sort the beans and things like that. I was having trouble seeing people unless they were wearing white clothes. I could not tell the difference between colours.

Maria did not have her 1,000 francs with her when she was prescribed the glasses. But the outreach registrar allowed her to keep them on condition that she paid for them later.

She was relieved and looked forward to going back to cultivating. 'Nothing can be impossible to me. I will be able to sort out crops. I will be able to look in the distance and see who a person is and how they are dressed.'

By now, night in the Rwandan hills was beginning to fall and the team had to leave for the long drive back. That potholed track would be no easier in the dark.

Lightning pierced the skies as a thunderstorm erupted, making the journey back down to Kigali an interesting experience. It was a day of days, moving and inspirational, as hard-working nurses brought relief and happiness to people who had wondered if they could ever be helped.

A Postscript from the Hills

That was not the end of the story. The Clearly team went back to Maria a few weeks later to see how she was getting on. And oh, what a transformation!

The first thing they noticed was that the glasses had become so valuable to Maria that she was scared she might break them. She used them while walking and working at home, but not when she was cultivating because she feared they might fall from her eyes.

She said:

> I really value them and treat them very well, the way someone might treat their own child. I use them carefully so they last longer. I am poor and I would not be able to get another pair of glasses quickly if these ones did not even last a year.

Maria could hardly contain her enthusiasm.

> I value my glasses because they have helped me see what I could not see before. They have helped me sort out my crops. Glasses mean I can recognise someone when I might have hesitated before. I am now able to see somebody and recognise them without asking who they are.

They have made her a happier person. 'I can now freely talk with others. We laugh and we enjoy time together because

I am able to see and recognise everything and everyone around me. When you see others and talk to them and enjoy it, you feel happy.'

There is also a bit more leisure time.

With the extra time I get using my glasses to complete my chores quickly, I choose to go anywhere my feet can take me. I socialise with other people without any sense of hurry and without worrying that if I go home late I will have trouble seeing.

So a life has changed. 'I am now able to see clearly,' said Maria, which was music to the ears of the Clearly Team.

And she then summed up what my campaign is all about.

The reason I would wish everyone to be able to access glasses is because I got them and they are so important to me. If others got them, it would help them as it has helped me. I will not get old with vision problems. Instead I will see clearly. And all the others the nurses can help will be able to grow old seeing clearly as well.

Thank you, Maria. Your story is an inspiration to me and everyone connected with the Clearly campaign.

CHAPTER 3

THE FOUR Ds: OBSTACLES TO PROGRESS

The last 150 years have seen massive advances in public health. Early in the twentieth century, people in their thousands were dying from diseases like smallpox, diphtheria and even measles. Later in the century, thousands died from poliomyelitis. Vaccines for all of these diseases were developed, saving lives, and in some cases the diseases were eliminated altogether.

There have been similar advances in family planning. Overall fertility in the developing countries declined by a third from the 1960s through the 1980s, from an average of six children down to four, with dramatic decreases occurring in some parts of the world.

Herculean efforts continue, quite rightly, to halt the spread of malaria, HIV/Aids and tuberculosis.

But why has it taken until nearly 700 years after the invention of glasses for us to start thinking about all those billions of people who cannot see properly for want of vision screening and a pair of spectacles? It is almost as if no one thought about it until recently. Quite rightly, blindness has been the preoccupation of the world's health authorities and individual governments. But dealing with the simple problems of short- and long-sightedness by the provision of glasses has not been on people's radar for long. It is a surprising omission, but one that we and organisations like us are now seeking to put right.

Rwanda, as we have just seen, shows that there are ways to make great progress, particularly when the local conditions are helpful. In Rwanda, there is only one ophthalmologist for every million people, but nurses and health workers are empowered to deliver services that would otherwise have to be carried out by highly trained professionals.

No one in the eye health world knows more than Brian Doolan about the issues I am trying to highlight. Brian runs the wonderful Fred Hollows Foundation, which is based in Australia and has helped millions suffering from vision problems all over the developing world. He is a man who does not run away from controversy and has never been afraid to say what he thinks. In a recent conversation, he accused some eye health professionals of behaving like a 'medieval cabal' and declared that the prices charged for cataract operations in many countries were 'a scandal'. He does not mince his words.

I quote Brian early on because his outspoken comment goes to the heart of one of the key barriers to providing universal access to eye care.

As we went through our first year of the Clearly campaign, we concluded that the four biggest hurdles standing in the way of helping the neglected 2.5 billion were: diagnosis, distribution, dollars and demand – the four Ds.

If I can summarise, not enough people are authorised to deliver sight tests and prescribe glasses in the developing world, and lots of people do not know they have a problem (the diagnosis barrier); if they do know they have a problem, they can't get the glasses (the distribution barrier); or if they can get them, they cannot afford to buy them (the dollars barrier); and then, even if all those barriers are taken down, they may not want to wear them (the demand barrier).

On top of these barriers are the institutional biases relegating vision correction to the bottom of the pile, making it the problem that the world forgot.

Later in the book, I will give you my proposals for tackling all the Ds.

But first, let's take them all and explain them one by one.

Diagnosis

Brian's remark hit the button of the diagnosis problem. The overwhelming majority of the world's ophthalmologists and optometrists are in the developed world; the overwhelming majority of those who need their help are elsewhere. The figures are startling. Some 99 per cent of all ophthalmologists and optometrists live outside low-income countries. If you include lower middle-income countries, the figures are 83 per cent for ophthalmologists and 89 per cent for optometrists. But there has always been a perhaps understandable opposition among the professionals to seeing the jobs they have trained to do for years being done by those further down the healthcare chain after much shorter training periods. It is part of a constant striving for perfection. But it does not help those who are crying out for help. And, as the reader will see later, a company's attempt to allow people to do their own tests using a mobile phone app has met with big resistance from the professionals.

Even worse, the relatively tiny number of professionals in the developing world tend to live – again, understandably – in the big cities. It means, as I reveal in some of the case studies in this book, that people suffering from serious eye problems may have to walk miles to get to see a specialist.

Take this case. Dr Andrew Bastawrous, the founder of Peek Vision to whom I referred in the first chapter, told the heart-warming story at an awards event of Maria, a young Kenyan mother of three who'd walked for miles after hearing a rumour that an eye clinic was taking place. He went on:

When we examined her, we found that she was blind in both eyes.

She doesn't remember how old she was when she could last see, but she had faint memories of vision in her childhood. So, we took her to our clinic and we performed cataract surgery for her. We removed the clouded lenses from her eyes and replaced them with artificial lenses – and the next day she could see.

The effect was dramatic, because not only did she regain her sight, but she regained her dignity. She looked younger, she stood tall; and then she told us that we had a problem: she didn't know where she lived.

We had to try and find her home based on her memories, based on people who may know her; it took us hours to find her village. As we approached and got close, she became hesitant. She was worried that she didn't know what her husband looked like, and she didn't know what her children looked like.

Eventually, when we arrived, her husband was there, a farmer surrounded by children who were playing. But Maria didn't know which were hers – until her three children ran and embraced her.

All over the developing world there are stories like the miracle of Maria. And for her it was a miracle. But all she needed was a straightforward operation. And she was fortunate that Andrew and his team happened to choose that part of the world to hold their clinic. There will be similar stories as we go through this book.

As EYElliance, a coalition of eye-care NGOs, said in a groundbreaking report to the World Economic Forum in

2016, a shortage of eye-health workers combined with local laws stipulating that only professionals can prescribe and dispense glasses represent key barriers to adequately addressing the unmet need for glasses.[7]

As Jordan Kassalow, founder of VisionSpring, told me, there is strong opposition within the profession to task-shifting. In some countries in the developing world there might only be two ophthalmologists, but they are the ones most opposed to opening up the system to allow others to prescribe.

> In America and the United Kingdom, reading glasses are a consumer product and you can buy them in shops. It makes no sense that in countries where there is one ophthalmologist to 10,000 people, glasses are a consumer product, whereas in countries where there might be one ophthalmologist to 1 million people, they are prevented from acquiring them easily.

Why should this be?

The establishment maintains that allowing people to buy their glasses from someone other than an optometrist or ophthalmologist will put the public at risk because it might 'distract the public from regular eye examinations'.

At first glance, this argument seems reasonable, but when you scratch the surface it becomes clear that this is a coercive tactic that does not help the public image of the eye-care professions: conflating 'vision correction' with 'eye health' undermines the professionalism of the people working in eye care and it causes massive inflation of prices for eyewear.

First, let's address the issue of eye health examinations. Regular examinations of eye health (i.e. when an eye specialist looks at and inside your eyes to assess your health) are vital not only to look for conditions that may lead to blindness but also because the eye is a subtle barometer of general health, and is quickly affected by systemic diseases. A professional can pick up all manner of serious health issues including diabetes, hypertension, tumours, infections etc. Regular examinations of eye health are important. The question is whether restricting the sale of glasses is an effective way of ensuring that people get regular eye examinations.

Put simply, the people who argue against deregulation on this basis subscribe to the belief that restricting access to corrective eyewear is the best means of forcing the public to have their eyes examined more frequently. This is a coercive approach – and one that has failed in almost every public health initiative in which it has been applied, whether for the management of hypertension, obesity, diabetes or alcohol abuse. Indeed, when it comes to matters of public health and the means by which large-scale behavioural change is enacted, it is generally recognised that coercive paternalism is a poor tactic.

Rather, there is growing consensus that eye examination frequency is increased by efforts to educate consumers about the health benefits of obtaining comprehensive eye examinations at regular intervals. Notable examples of such campaigns include the National Eye Health Education Programme, the Think About Your Eyes campaign and the EyeSmart campaign. It is worth noting that none of these education efforts attempt to coerce patients into getting eye examinations by withholding access to corrective eyewear.

Responsibility for educating the general public about the health benefits of regular eye examinations rests with the profession itself. If it has been unable to do so until now then it is a failure of the profession that must be addressed. Regrettably, this noble task is understandably hampered by the dual role that optometry plays in our society. On the one hand, the eye-care professionals are learned people tasked with testing our eyesight and, on the other hand, they rely for their income almost exclusively on the commercial activity of selling the eyeglasses they prescribe. Almost all their revenue comes from the sale of glasses, and very little of their income comes from examining the health of the eye.

That this dual role exists is not a bad thing in and of itself. Indeed, there are many sound practical reasons to house both roles under one roof – not the least of which is sheer convenience for the consumer. Nevertheless, the difficulty comes because this dual role is protected by trade regulations. Protection of this sort means that the sale of corrective eyewear need not be subject to free-market pressures... and that means that prices will be inflated. What I would argue for in my ideal world is the deregulation of the trade of measuring the power of the eye and selling the glasses to correct it. Furthermore, I would argue for even stronger regulation of the professional act of examining the health of the eye, and call on regulators, trade bodies and the health sector to improve public education of the benefits of regular examinations of eye health.

Essentially, the current structure of the industry is such that they're paid for their trade, not their profession. This must change – and it can change – through task-shifting.

Distribution

Most of our 2.5 billion in need of glasses live in parts of the world that are difficult to reach. And within those countries, millions live in villages that are not accessible by normal transport. During the wet seasons, the tracks, such as they are, become impassable. For some, the local town may be 50–60 kilometres away and the only way to get there is on foot. Some of them never see their local town, let alone go to the shops there. So getting glasses to the people who need them is difficult, even if they know they have a problem. Shops that sell everyday items like Coca-Cola, bread and cornflakes do not as a matter of course stock glasses, the kind we can buy off the shelf in Boots in the UK.

Part of the problem is the lengthy supply chain. A typical chain for reading glasses is manufacture, transport to the recipient country, the payment of import taxes and duties, then a regional distributor, usually storing the glasses in a warehouse somewhere, then on to a local distributor and then sale. Lens and frames for prescription glasses follow a similar but longer path. After reaching the local distributor we then have to take account of transport, then the opticians, then possibly more transport to the laboratory for fitting of lens to frame, and then sale. All the way along the line, someone, somewhere, has to take their cut, and the price rises each time.

And the stories of organisations that have worked for a long time in this field show how the pricing structure makes it hard to advance.

Shortly after founding VisionSpring in 2003, Jordan Kassalow recruited and trained local women in Hyderabad in India and Santa Ana in El Salvador to sell reading glasses to their communities. The vision entrepreneurs, as they were called, earned a commission from each sale and were expected to build a small business from which they could earn a living. They were taught how to diagnose presbyopia.

But as a report by Stanford Business School on the story of VisionSpring[8] made clear, it turned out that getting to break-even was more difficult than expected. VisionSpring generated $3 of revenue per pair of glasses, net of commission. The cost of goods, including manufacturing them in China and transporting them to local warehouses, was $1.50 per pair. So, although it had gross margins in the 50 per cent range, it had significant management expenses to cover, including the cost of local staff who had to recruit and manage the vision entrepreneurs. That gives us some idea of the delivery challenges.

Online glasses retailers are turning the traditional method of selling glasses on its head and as a result can offer their wares at a fraction of the cost. It goes without saying that they are experiencing tremendous resistance from the establishment.

There it is. If you're living in a part of the world where you have to go to an optical store to purchase your glasses then you must expect to pay for a business model that was probably last fit for purpose in the late nineteenth century.

We should instead encourage the search for new and exciting methods of selling and distributing glasses in the developing world that will challenge the traditional approach to doing business – perhaps even bypassing the need for much of the infrastructure that the developed world is stuck with. It is not unreasonable to think that this might happen – think of how the rise of cell phones made the need for costly telephone networks obsolete in many African countries.

Ultimately, whatever approach offers the greatest perceived value and convenience to the end user will win out. Who knows, perhaps the business models for selling glasses that gain traction in the developing world will someday make their way back into the developed world, meaning we can all pay a little less for our eyewear.

Dollars

All the difficulties I have highlighted so far combine to make the third D – keeping the cost of glasses affordable for people in the developing countries – all the more difficult to tackle.

Here, the structure of the industry poses a problem. It is one where the 'mark-up' in prices from manufacture to sale is high. There are two big players in the prescription glasses field: Luxottica, responsible for the frames, and Essilor, for the lenses. They dominate the industry and they are merging.

Let me explain. There are two main categories of spectacles: prescription glasses, which contain lenses customised to the needs of the individual, and reading glasses, which are not made for any particular person.

Prescription glasses can contain negative or positive lenses. Negative lenses are thin in the middle and thicker at the edges; they minify objects and are used to correct short-sightedness. Positive lenses are thick in the middle and thinner at the edges; they magnify objects and are used to correct far-sightedness. Reading glasses always have positive lenses, and although they can be used by some far-sighted people to see distant objects clearly, they are intended mainly for people suffering from presbyopia, blurred near vision, which usually occurs in the over-forties.

So let's have a look at the mark-ups, using US prices. Frames for prescription glasses can be made for between $2 and $7.[9] At the time of import they will cost on average $11 but vary between $3 and anything up to $100.[10] By the time they are purchased by the end user, frames can typically cost between $30 and $700.

The initial manufacturing cost for lenses is only a few cents. At this stage they are called 'lens pucks' and are not usable until technical work has been done on them. The average cost of import into the US was $2.85 in 2016 and they can be bought by optometrists for between $3 and $10.[11] The average price of a lens sold in the US in 2016 was $130,[12] but could cost as little as $30 and as much as $400.

Reading glasses are a low-margin game. They can cost as little as $0.50 to make, with lenses and frames combined, but they are not great products. Good ones cost between $2 and $5 to produce. They will typically retail for between $5 and $20.

The two manufacturing streams – reading and prescription – are worlds apart. So the big mark-up is an integral feature of the prescription glasses market. That obviously creates problems when the market we are aiming to help is the developing world, where in many parts the average daily income per head is no more than $2.

In countries like Rwanda and Bangladesh, where Vision-Spring and VFAN subsidise the overall cost in the interests of creating a market, the customers are more fortunate than those where they do not benefit from subsidies.

In Uganda, the excellent Light for the World development organisation has been involved for several years in a campaign to correct refractive errors. It is the failure of world authorities to tackle the problem of uncorrected refractive errors that is at the heart of the Clearly campaign. Its customers pay a flat fee the equivalent of $8.20 for glasses whatever the individual needs. This keeps the price manageable for what would otherwise be much more expensive prescription glasses. A third of the cash is kept by the eye department in the hospital or health centre that served the patient and the other two-thirds goes to the national optical workshop at Entebbe General Hospital. Light for the World subsidises staff overhead costs.

But move away from the subsidised model in Uganda and you get an idea of the mark-ups involved in this industry. Spectacles are usually only found in the bigger cities but often the starting price for simple corrective lenses with a cheap frame is around $41 and can go up to $55.

Highly powered lenses are even more expensive, and simple, ready-made reading glasses are around $20 to $25 at optical centres. Street vendors may charge from around $10 after bargaining. But bear in mind the wholesale buying price for these basic spectacles is about $3. So money is being made along the line.

Vision Aid Overseas supports setting up vision centres in Zambia and four other African countries, which help to provide free eye tests and affordable glasses (lowest price $4 per pair) to all, including the poorest consumers. Sometimes frames and lenses are donated by organisations like

Specsavers UK and Essilor, but most often they are bought using the income generated by the vision centres, through charging more for people who can afford them in the effort to leave a sustainable market behind.

If they are subsidised by organisations like VisionSpring, glasses arrive in countries like Rwanda at a cost of less than half a dollar. But those prices treble when transport costs and sales commission are considered.

The truth is that there is no true open market in glasses in either the developed or the developing world. Yes, some countries, like Britain, allow you to buy your reading glasses over the counter in Boots. But the sale of prescription glasses virtually everywhere is protected and subject to being prescribed by a professional. Which makes them many times more expensive, too expensive for families in the developing countries. And the totally unintended consequence of this policy is that hundreds of millions of children are having to go without vision correction. I would contend that there is little difference between reading and prescription glasses.

In simple terms, 500 million people need only reading glasses; 1.65 billion need only distance glasses; and a further 350 million need both readers and distance spectacles. Getting reading glasses to all of these people would take a big slice out of this problem; getting prescription glasses to all would smash it to pieces.

Finally, import duties and taxes often stand in the way of providing affordable glasses in the developing countries. In countries such as Bangladesh, they are very high. Such duties inhibit entrepreneurs, who are already only guaranteed a small profit margin on the goods they sell.

As David Chute, who is on the board of both VisionSpring and RestoringVision, another not-for-profit distributor of glasses, told me: 'We are trying to improve the intelligence, productivity and quality of people's lives in these countries. Why these governments would tax us and make it hard is simply mind-boggling.'

Demand

When talking about demand, we must accept that even now in some developing countries there is an aversion to spectacles, a stigma somehow that they imply weakness, a fear that they detract from one's natural looks. For our campaign to work, people must understand that they have an eye problem and then want to put it right. Wearing glasses should not be seen as uncool. So we still have cultural barriers to break down there. Even in Rwanda, the take-up by people prescribed glasses is far lower than it should be, and they have a President who proudly sports his glasses at every opportunity.

Glasses are still not seen as a necessity in less developed countries. Consumers do not fully understand the problem, or the value in solving it, or that a product exists to solve it. This phenomenon was highlighted in the EYElliance report. Potential customers are often unaware that they have a correctable problem. Others do not know that an existing simple solution can help them see clearly, increase their productivity and improve their quality of life. Culturally based stigmas only exacerbate this barrier to procuring glasses, as misperceptions persist about their benefits.

Unlike things that consumers readily desire and demand, a product like glasses requires establishing a loyal following and convincing consumers of its value. EYElliance pointed out that in contrast to solar lights, ovens and mobile phones, the value of glasses has not been adequately explained to low-income consumers, particularly if they have to meet the travel costs of getting screened if they are outside urban areas.

Thus, solutions that involve issuing prescriptions for eyeglasses have lower acquisition rates than those that deliver glasses at the point of care after a screening. The answer is: take glasses to them.

When he tried VisionSpring's vision entrepreneur model, training local women to sell reading glasses to their communities, Jordan Kassalow found it was hampered by the fact that customers often did not grasp how their lives could change with reading glasses. The impact of vision loss was less visceral than things like river blindness, an infection spread by a blackfly that breeds in rapidly flowing streams. Besides this, many customers did not know why they should trust the entrepreneurs and had a 'one day you are my neighbour and the next you are an eye doctor' reaction to them.

The Stanford report that said cultural factors also played a strong role. In India, up to 70 per cent of women of marriageable age believed that their marriage prospects would be dimmed if they wore glasses. Women who wore them feared being perceived to have genetic and/or physical defects.

So there we have the four Ds – the big obstacles to progress as we try to help the world see. They are the barriers we have to break down, and later I will set out my proposals to deal with each of them.

CHAPTER 4

COUNTING THE COST

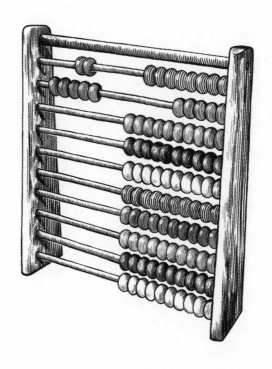

Spending money on improving people's sight makes good economic sense – in fact, it's a no-brainer.

In the public mind, the words 'poor sight' instantly conjure images of conditions that require complicated medical interventions. These conditions, which affect 165 million people – things like cataracts, glaucoma, macular degeneration and others – automatically make vision a problem that should be left to the 'experts'. It is little wonder then that almost all efforts have been directed towards these issues, and almost no attention has been paid to the 2.5 billion who cannot see properly.

But, but, but... The world cost of visual impairment, including both blindness and refractive error, is some $3 trillion a year.

It is the figure that we cite when urging governments and international authorities to act.

The most authoritative calculation of this mammoth cost came in *Global Public Health*, an international journal for research, policy and practice, in 2012.[13]

It estimated that the total cost of visual impairment globally was $3 trillion in 2010, of which $2.3 trillion was direct health costs. This burden is projected to increase by approximately 20 per cent by 2020.

By direct health costs, we mean the cost of dealing with eye problems in national health programmes – inpatient and outpatient services, pharmaceuticals, glasses and emergency care. The remaining $0.7 trillion covers lost productivity, tax and welfare spending, and informal care.

Vision impairment is associated with a considerable disease burden. Unless steps are taken to reduce prevalence through prevention and treatment, this burden will increase alongside global population growth, the report found.

So, what do we make of that figure? Well, for a start, it's crazy that no one seems to have woken up to it. The same study finds that poor vision costs the global economy $168 billion in lost productivity alone. And we should add to this welfare and tax losses of $238 billion and informal care costs of $246 billion.

The $3 trillion cost is nearly half of what we spend on healthcare globally.[14] It's a problem that affects more of us than any other disability and, left untreated, hinders our ability to get an education, support our families and build a better life.

As we've seen, people with poor vision can be divided into roughly two groups: the 5 per cent who need surgery and special medication to deal with diseases like glaucoma and cataracts and the 95 per cent who need little more than a pair of glasses to see well enough to go about their daily lives independently and productively.

That crude division is not reflected in the structure of the industry that has, over the past few centuries, evolved to tackle poor vision: 200,000 ophthalmologists to manage eye diseases and surgery; 170,000 optometrists to take care of the glasses and contact lenses. There are more than enough specialists to tackle the vision problems of the world. The World Health Organization has set a target of at least one ophthalmologist for every 250,000 people; that's approximately 30,000 ophthalmologists globally. The world has 200,000, but the proportion based in the developing world is tiny.

The WHO target also calls for at least one optometrist for every 50,000 people: that's approximately 150,000 optometrists globally. We have 170,000.

Unfortunately, none of this helps if you live in a developing country, because 99 per cent of these specialists live in parts of the world where they are able to earn the income their training, skill and expertise demand.

So that is our problem. The traditional model is fantastic, but only if you can afford to access it. It may be possible to take the traditional model, with all its experts, facilities and equipment, and seed it in the parts of the world where it is needed most, but the latest estimate suggests that you'd need to train an army of 65,000 eye-care providers and build and equip 50,000 facilities at a price of $50,000 each. This amounts to $28 billion if you are catering for all those who need glasses. If you include those with eye diseases, you're looking at something in the region of an additional $128 billion.

$128 billion may not seem like much when this problem costs the global economy $3 trillion a year. But you start to get a sense of the scale of the challenge in funding this effort when you consider that the world's top eye-care NGOs and charities – working under the auspices of the WHO – collectively have only about $850 million a year to work with, as I explained earlier.

Regrettably, the prospect of being able to raise $128 billion for vision correction seems highly unlikely when you consider that the total global development funding for health – focused mainly on life-threatening conditions like malaria and HIV/Aids – amounted to $36 billion in 2015.[15]

And yet all the economics point to action. Studies have shown that every dollar put into dealing with this problem produces a handsome return on investment. Providing affordable glasses has been shown to boost productivity by up to 34 per cent among rural agricultural workers.[16] A recent study has shown that providing glasses to primary school students boosts test scores. In some cases, the improved performance is equivalent to between one third and a half-year of extra schooling.[17]

Research by the Fred Hollows Foundation showed that for every $1 invested in preventing someone from going blind, at least four times the financial benefit goes to the economy.[18]

As VisionSpring pointed out in a recent report, the return on investment in a pair of glasses is high. A pair of reading glasses can increase individual productivity by 34 per cent, and VisionSpring's further analysis of data from north India suggests that this can translate to a 20 per cent average increase in a wearer's annual income.[19]

It's not as though these people need some as yet unheard of technology to tap into their potential. What they need is access to a technology that has been available to us for over 700 years.

Money is not the root of all evil. Comparatively modest investment – and, as the figures show, it is an investment – would help the economies of dozens of countries, and billions of individuals.

Surely, when they are deciding how to spend limited public funds, governments should consider that giving everyone the right to vision screening must have knock-on economic benefits. It has to make sense to prioritise in this area.

CASE STUDY I

THEOPHILLE

Theophille Ingabire was on her daily two-hour walk to work from her home in Kabuye to a textile factory in Kigali, the capital of Rwanda, when disaster struck.

All of us who wear glasses have experienced that moment of panic when we put our spectacles down somewhere and can't find them, often precisely because we can't see as well without them. We fear being late for work, or even having to go to work without them. How will we cope?

For Theophille, it was much, much worse than that. She lost her glasses – they probably fell from her pocket – and she was never to see them again.

Those glasses were Theophille's lifeline. They had kept her in her job at Rwanda's only textile factory, a job she desperately needed to help support her four children. Like millions of Africans, she walks everywhere – there is no alternative – and for years she had walked four hours a day – two hours there, and two hours back – to be able to work.

Today, Theophille is a tailor, threading the needles on an embroidery machine attached to a computer screen, and monitoring the machine as it sews names into the cloth. It is a responsible, difficult job requiring abilities to read and write, precise handiwork and, most important, good eyesight.

But I am getting ahead of myself. Back then, Theophille was a supervisor at the factory. It was her job to read and check the names of workers for the daily roll-call. She did it for fourteen years, but while doing this equally vision-dependent job, something started to go wrong with her eyes. She could only see the names on the sheet by holding it at arm's length. She began to get dizzy and her eyes often itched and felt as if they were burning.

So, in January 2012, her local health centre referred her to a Kigali hospital, where, after a series of vision tests, she was told the problem was due to bacteria in her eyes; she was given two kinds of eye drops. They did not seem to work and after two weeks she returned to the hospital for further tests and was prescribed reading glasses. Because she had health insurance, they cost her the equivalent of $8, still almost a month of savings for Theophille.

At first, as she got used to them, the glasses made Theophille feel slightly dizzy, but the sensation wore off and soon her ability to read and write was fully restored, along with her confidence.

Then, devastation. She lost them.

Let's switch now to St Mary's Catholic Church in Kabuye on a Sunday morning in February 2017.

Sitting at the back in a congregation of about 1,200 people were members of the Clearly team who had gone to Rwanda to look at the work of my Vision for a Nation organisation, the charity I established to try to bring nationwide screening to the country.

It was a happy service as the parents of Kabuye and their children participated fully and joyfully in the prayers and hymns.

Towards the end of the ninety-minute gathering, a bespectacled woman with an air of authority went to the lectern and delivered speedily and with confidence a series of announcements about events at the church over the coming few days, telling her listeners how various saints' days would be marked. She went on for several minutes, scarcely pausing for breath.

It was Theophille, a smiling and obviously happy Theophille.

How did this come to pass? After that black day when she lost her first pair of glasses, she tried to replace them at another hospital but the cost, six times the original, was impossible for her to meet, with the demands of looking after her family having to come first. It would have taken the next four months to save the money.

Then, seven months later, Theophille was told by a colleague whose wife worked at the local health centre that there were now trained nurses there who could screen people for eye problems and that if they found you needed glasses you could buy them for as little as $1.50, or 1,000 Rwandan francs.

Theophille went to the Kinyinya health centre as fast as her legs could take her there. A trained nurse conducted the same vision tests she had had done at the hospital previously and she got her new glasses, vowing never to lose them again. Her life has been changed, at work and at home. She is confident, she is overjoyed.

Theophille's predicament, we now know, is shared by millions upon millions around the world. If you cannot see, you cannot learn or work effectively, perhaps at all. Poor vision is a huge barrier to securing and keeping a job; it shackles the potential of individuals and perpetuates the cycle of poverty.

Refractive error, which I will explain in detail in a later chapter, is the main cause of poor vision, but in 90 per cent of cases it can be dealt with by glasses. Theophille was one of those billions who had never had access to a proper eye test.

Theophille's life was changed, I'm happy to say, because Vision for a Nation, working with the Rwandan Ministry of Health, has been training nurses to provide primary eye care as part of the standard package of health services available to the country's residents.

After that church service, the Clearly team went with Theophille, now forty-six, to her home a few miles away to meet her husband Jean-Pierre and some of her children. She told them how getting her good vision back has enriched her life. 'After receiving the second pair of glasses, my life was so much better. I can read, I can write, I can do the household chores, I can see. It is wonderful but without them life was bad.'

Speaking of the time the problem emerged, she said:

It was the potential loss of reading that saddened me most. I was concerned that I would no longer be able to read even though I knew how to read. At the church they also plan for me to read scripture or announcements each Sunday, or at least once a month. At work I would get something to read and I could not read it because I could not see.

She frowned as she remembered the fateful day when her first pair of glasses went missing. 'I was rushing for work – I don't know if I was late – and somewhere on the road they must have fallen from my jacket. It was terrible. I searched and I did not find them. I didn't see when or where they fell.'

To prevent it ever happening again, she keeps the new pair in a handbag and she has also acquired a pocket cover for them to prevent them from breaking.

She smiles when she recounts how having glasses again has enriched her life.

Theophille said: 'The glasses have helped me in my Christian life because I can read the word of God to the congregation and pray using them as well.'

She can also help her children with their homework again.

Her visitors told her how impressed they had been at the church service. 'Yes, when I have glasses I can read very fluently. Without them, I cannot read.'

One happy customer for VFAN and the Ministry of Health. One of many across the world whose lives have been changed through getting glasses.

CHAPTER 5

THE GOLDEN THREAD THROUGH THE GLOBAL GOALS

Eye health did not rate a mention in the United Nations' seventeen sustainable development goals (SDGs) or in their associated 169 targets and 241 indicators adopted in 2015. These goals were the benchmark for all UN states to frame their agendas and political policies over the following fifteen years.

Each goal defines specific targets, supposedly offering key steps forward to ensure the tangible realisation of the human rights enshrined in the UN's original declaration of 1948.

From 'eradicating extreme poverty for all people everywhere' to 'ending all forms of discrimination against all women and girls everywhere' to 'ensuring that all girls and boys complete free, equitable and quality primary and secondary education', the goals aspire to phenomenal global progression.

But laying out cross-border policy priorities for the world's leaders and institutions is a major task. Too often, the macro-level approach of these agenda-setting summits means that vital issues fail to make it on to the global agenda.

Poor vision is one such issue. And I would call that blurred vision on the part of world leaders. This issue is too urgent to wait for the next batch of development goals, whenever they may be.

It is a huge pity, but it reflects the reality that eye problems are further down the list of priorities in the eyes of governments and aid donors than the killer diseases. Despite the massive number of people affected and the huge cost to the economy, poor vision is considered non-urgent and tends to drop off the scale when measured against life-threatening communicable epidemics such as HIV, Ebola and malaria, all of which are directly referenced in the SDGs.

The drive to treat poor vision has historically failed to hit the global policy agenda and therefore attract funding, innovation and investment. As a result, there has been little advance in our approach to vision since the humble pair of spectacles was first invented.

But as Clearly embarks on a programme of advocacy to highlight the economic and quality of life costs of 2.5 billion people not being able to see properly, we and organisations in our sphere will be working hard to show that many of those goals cannot be achieved without a worldwide boost to eye care.

Failing to tackle poor vision is preventing global humanitarian agencies from making headway on the UN's goals. In particular, poor vision is hampering progress in the fight to reduce global poverty and income disparity and to ensure access to educational opportunities for all.

A team of specialists visited a cotton spinning and textile factory in Madurai, south India. A series of eyesight tests revealed that around 80 per cent unknowingly suffered from poor vision. Those in need of vision correction were provided with prescription glasses and just one month later 44 per cent of the spinners demonstrated a marked increase in productivity. Current rates of poor vision are a crippling impediment to the economic growth of developing countries.

Good eyesight is the golden thread running through many of the UN's main development goals. For example, Goal 4 asks governments to ensure inclusive quality education and lifelong learning opportunities. We will be arguing that avoidable blindness and refractive errors must have an impact on education and attainment standards.

Access to good-quality education helps people escape from poverty and boosts long-term economic development. Like health, it should be a universal right. But if you are at school and cannot see the board or read from the textbook, your life chances will be heavily affected. In 2013, there were 59 million children of primary school age out of school and of these it was estimated one third lived with a disability, including blindness or visual impairment. As long as vision problems remain unaddressed, millions of people across the globe will be prevented from accessing the benefits of education, even where the resources are available to them.

And of course Goal 5, which tells governments to achieve gender equality and empower all women, is an issue that the Clearly campaign is determined to highlight. There is nothing very equal about eye problems. Two thirds of those suffering vision impairment are women. In many developing countries, women are far less likely to be able to leave their villages for treatment and far more likely to contract a communicable eye disease, often from their children. The WHO has noted that women have less access to eye treatment and healthcare than men, due to a lack of transport to care providers and a lack of finances to pay for their services.

Then there is Goal 8 – to promote economic growth and create decent work for all. The impact of poor vision can be immediate and long-lasting and affects the future of the whole family. When someone cannot see clearly at work, they are more likely to injure themselves or someone else and cannot work to their full potential. The high international cost of poor vision has been referred to throughout this book. So helping the world to see clearly can only assist in achieving Goal 8.

Clear vision is essential to Goal 10, too, which urges governments to reduce inequalities, including the terrible inequality that disability inevitably inflicts, as well as Goal 1, to end poverty. There can be few things more likely to help individuals and countries escape from the grip of poverty than the ability of people to see clearly to work, to study, to drive and to play a full part in family life.

Our thinking here is in line with our fellow campaigners EYElliance. Co-founder Jordan Kassalow told me that in setting it up he had tried to build a multi-stakeholder ecosystem aimed at placing vision issues more centrally on the economic development agenda. The aim was to get governments, the private sector and civic society working together to solve the problem on a global basis through all means possible, including showing the importance of good vision to education, road safety, financial inclusion and other issues.

The 2016 EYElliance report for the World Economic Forum contrasted the treatment of poor vision in developed and developing worlds. In the developed countries, most of those whose vision could be improved with a pair of glasses are able to obtain an eye test and affordable glasses either through public health systems or private-sector opticians and online optical companies, or at pharmacies and shops if they only need a pair of reading glasses. With a pair of glasses obtained relatively easily, their vision is restored and the problem solved, thus eliminating the disadvantages associated with persistently poor vision.

Contrast that with the vast majority, some 80 per cent, of those without access to affordable, properly prescribed glasses, who live in less developed countries with limited qualitative and affordable eye-care options. Unlike other public health problems, however, unequal access to the solution is not the result of costly medical treatment.

No, the current unmet need for glasses in developing countries stems from neglect. For many years, a lack of epidemiological data resulted in inaccurate sizing of the affected population. Without data and statistics, governments face a challenge in allocating the necessary resources to address such a problem.

Prior to 2008, the World Health Organization was collecting data only on the number of individuals whose vision could be restored with medical interventions. As a result, governments and the global health community had robust data on how many people needed surgery and medical treatment, but no information on the number of people in need of a pair of glasses.

Without clarity on the scope of the problem, governments did not commit adequate resources to train eye health workers, nor did they fully integrate the identification of poor vision and correction of vision with glasses into public health systems. So yes, we would have liked the UN to have been bolder – much bolder.

This is an urgent problem and it should have been addressed directly in those goals.

Peter Ackland, chief executive of the International Agency for the Prevention of Blindness (IAPB) and a strong supporter of Clearly, takes a more positive attitude than we do to the goals despite the absence of a direct reference to eye care. We saw him in his office near Russell Square, London and he recited the goals and their sub-clauses to emphasise how eye health campaigners have plenty to work on as they try to squeeze more from governments, corporations and aid agencies.

For example, the catch-all category of health and well-being is Goal 3. It urges countries to 'ensure healthy lives and promote well-being for all at all ages'. Well, I'm sure no one would argue with that. But, as Peter said, sub-clause 8, calling for universal health coverage and affordable care for the poorest, is already being used by his organisation and others like ours to push the case for eye health to be included. 'Our objective is to ensure that eye health is included in this essential healthcare package and I am optimistic that it will be,' he told us.

Another sub-clause emphasises the need for training essential parts of the health workforce, and the IAPB and others are pressing for eye health workers to be included there too.

Discussions are taking place to decide which indicators will be used to measure the coverage of essential health services as set out in the goals. The WHO and the World Bank have suggested a small number of core treatment and preventative health interventions.

Peter confirmed that although cataract surgery was not included in the original list, the IAPB is working hard to present the case that it should be. He has been to the World Bank and WHO to argue his brief and, while not counting chickens, is hopeful that he might succeed. If so, that would be a boost, although we would want refractive error to be included as well.

As Peter said:

It would be a major breakthrough. But it is not as if there are not solutions. There are: routine operations for cataracts and glasses for refractive errors. It's affordable. It's not rocket science. People will want easy wins when they need to show how they are measuring up against the targets. Well, if this leads to a boost in eye care around the world, we will all be winners.

Peter is a big supporter of our aims. 'The more organisations who are out there drawing attention to the problems of eye disease and refractive errors the better,' he told me.

He does not believe it is a case of governments or corporations failing to 'get' the impact of poor eyesight on their economies.

'To be honest, it is about competing priorities. Poor eyesight does not cause you to die and many of these countries are combatting diseases that do cause you to die. It is a fact of life.'

He suggests the productivity argument should be used, but it should be used as one tool in a bag of many and it should be used carefully.

To be frank, most ministers in these countries have heard it before. They get people going in and saying 'for every dollar you put into primary and secondary education you get ten out', or 'for every dollar you spend to combat this disease you get fourteen out'. Our mantra is that for every dollar spent on cataract surgery you get four back.

And for many of these guys they are not interested in the money that may come down the road. I remember an African minister telling me that he was more interested in balancing the books this year than any gain he might make in many years' time. This is the reality of it all.

Peter allocates no particular blame for the world eyesight problem on the big lens and frame companies.

Obviously their priority has been selling in the developed world, where people are prepared to pay big sums for a pair of specs. That is business. But they do sell in the developing world and if the demand is there – there is certainly a big market – they will take their opportunities.

It is good that Peter and his organisation will continue to fight the good fight for greater recognition of the vision problem. But it would have been so much better if it had been explicitly recognised rather than leaving people like Peter and us to look through the undergrowth of the clauses and sub-clauses to find crumbs of comfort.

We will continue to demand that the UN gives more explicit recognition to the importance of clear sight and the elimination of unavoidable blindness in its future deliberations and goals.

And we spent the summer of 2017 planning a visit to the UN General Assembly to make our case.

PART II

THE
SCIENCE

CHAPTER 6

THE MYSTERY OF THE HUMAN EYE

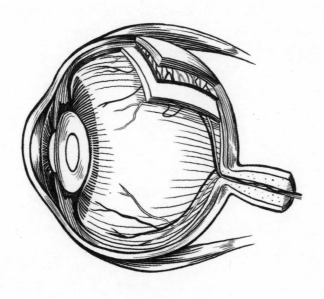

The eyes are our window to the world. This book is about trying to help everyone look through that window.

But first we have to understand one thing: the human eye is far from perfect. The eyes of many of our friends in the animal kingdom put our own to shame. The density of the light-sensing cells in the eye of the eagle is several times that in humans, meaning it can pick out its prey from long distances. Likewise the hawk.

As a superb article in *National Geographic*, in which it called the eye nature's most exquisite creation, told us, the box jellyfish has twenty-four eyes.[20] They are dark brown and grouped into four clusters called rhopalia. Scientist Dan-Eric Nilsson revealed that four of the six eyes in each rhopalium are simple light-detecting slits and pits. But the other two are surprisingly sophisticated, with light-focusing lenses, and can see images.

Why on earth should the dear old box jellyfish, with hardly a brain, need so many eyes? In 2007, Nilsson and his team demonstrated that it used its lower lensed eyes to spot approaching obstacles, like the mangrove roots that it swims among. It took them another four years to discover what the upper lensed eyes do. The first big clue was a free-floating weight at the bottom of the rhopalium that ensures that the upper eye is always looking upward, even if the jellyfish swims upside down. If this eye detects dark patches, the jellyfish senses that it's swimming beneath the mangrove canopy, where it can find the small crustaceans that it eats. If it sees only bright light, it has strayed into open water, and risks starving. With the help of its eyes, this brainless blob can find food, avoid obstacles and survive.

The author told us that the box jellyfish's eyes are part of an almost endless variation in the animal kingdom. Some see only in black and white; others perceive the full rainbow and beyond, to forms of light invisible to our eyes. Some can't even gauge the direction of incoming light; others can spot running prey miles away.

The smallest animal eyes, adorning the heads of fairy wasps, are barely bigger than an amoeba; the biggest are the size of dinner plates and belong to a gigantic squid species. The squid's eye, like ours, works as a camera does, with a single lens focusing light onto a single retina, full of photoreceptors – cells that absorb photons and convert their energy into an electrical signal.

By contrast, a fly's compound eye divides incoming light among thousands of separate units, each with its own lens and photoreceptors. Human, fly and squid eyes are mounted in pairs on their owners' heads. But scallops have rows of eyes along their mantles, starfish have eyes on the tips of their arms and the purple sea urchin's entire body acts as one big eye. There are eyes with bifocal lenses, eyes with mirrors, and eyes that look up, down and sideways all at the same time.

That's the animal eyes. Now what about our eyes and how they work?

We see when light reflected off an object passes into our eye through the cornea and pupil. Simple. But there are many parts of the eye, each of which can suffer from various problems.

There are two lenses in the eye. The first lens is the cornea, the transparent circular structure at the front of the eyeball that covers the coloured part of the eye. The second lens, the crystalline lens, is hidden behind the coloured part of the eye. These lenses have the job of focusing light on the light-sensitive cells that line the inside of the eye.

The coloured part of the eye is called the iris and it lies between the cornea and crystalline lens. Tiny muscles inside the iris control the amount of light entering the eye by opening (dilating) and closing (constricting) the hole in its centre, which is called the pupil. When there is a lot of light, the pupil is small. When it is dark, the pupil enlarges to allow more light in.

The layer of light-sensitive cells on the inside of the eye upon which the cornea and crystalline lens try to focus light is called the retina. The retina contains millions of photoreceptors that convert light into electric impulses, which travel from the retina to the brain along the optic nerve. Where the optic nerve leaves the retina, there are no sensory cells, which explains the blind spot.

So how does this mysterious organ work? Light reflects off objects and travels to the eye in a straight line until it comes across the cornea. The cornea bends – or refracts – the light and a portion of this refracted light then passes through the pupil to be refracted yet again by the crystalline lens. This light then travels to the photoreceptors of the retina to form an image. The photoreceptors convert light to electrical impulses, which travel along the optic nerve into the brain, which makes sense of it all and tells us what we see. Phew!

You would think that with such a complicated organ and set of tasks for each component part, things could go wrong, and they do – sometimes badly; sometimes in a simple way, which can be put right.

If the cornea and the crystalline lens work together to focus light on the retina – which works with the brain to give us vision – then we will see clearly.

Now, many people develop errors of refraction during childhood or later in life. Many develop imperfections of the cornea and lens, causing refracted light to be focused either in front of or behind the retina, making images blurry. People with refractive errors can still see colour and light, but the details of what they are looking at are often out of focus.

To put it as simply as possible, people with eyes that bring light to a focus in front of the retina suffer from a refractive error called myopia. People with eyes that focus light behind the retina suffer from hyperopia.

The key to dealing with these sorts of problems is refraction – the ability of a transparent medium, like glass, water or the eye, to change the direction of light travelling through it. And this is where the lenses come in. A person with myopia needs concave lenses to diverge the light rays entering the eye to 'push' the focal point backward onto the retina. Conversely, a person with hyperopia can use convex lenses to converge light rays entering the eye to 'pull' the focal point forwards onto the retina.

Using lenses to correct vision is not a new idea: the first mention of a lens being used to influence the focusing of light is in a joke told by Strepsiades to Socrates in Aristophanes' *The Clouds*. It is possible that lenses pre-date this, though; the oldest known object that could fit the bill is the Nimrud lens, which dates back to 750 BC Babylonia. However, it was not until more than 1,500 years later that the same principle would be used to create the earliest glasses.

That's the eye. What about the conditions that can affect it?

As we've seen, myopia is a condition of the eye where light is brought to a focus in front of the retina. This happens because either the curvature of the cornea or crystalline lens is too steep or the eyeball is too long.

Generally, short-sightedness happens when the eye continues to grow and becomes too long from front to back. As a result, light rays don't reach the retina at the back of the eye. They only focus in front of it. Myopes complain of having blurry vision when looking at things in the distance, but are able to see nearby objects clearly. It is for this reason that myopia is often referred to as short-sightedness.

Hyperopia is a condition of the eye in which light is brought to a focus behind the retina. It is usually caused by the curvature of the cornea or crystalline lens being too flat or the length of the eyeball being too short. The visual effects of hyperopia are not as straightforward as myopia, and depend to a large extend on a person's age. A fifty-year-old person will complain that objects in the distance are blurry and that nearby objects are even blurrier. A ten-year-old hyperope may not notice any blur whatsoever, but their clear vision will come at a cost: eye strain. Hyperopia is often referred to as far-sightedness and, much like near-sightedness, is caused by a combination of genetic and environmental factors.

Then there's astigmatism. Some people have a cornea or crystalline lens with a non-spherical shape that gives rise to a form of out-of-focus vision that makes all objects seem blurred, whether near or far. The ideal cornea should be shaped round like a football, but in cases of astigmatism it is shaped more like a rugby ball. This means that light rays entering the eye are not focused to a single point, creating a blurred image no matter where the eye is looking. In most cases, astigmatism is present at birth. However, it sometimes develops after an injury to the eye or as a complication of an eye operation.

As we age, the crystalline lens becomes harder and less elastic. This loss of elasticity reduces the eye's ability to focus sharply on nearby objects and reading glasses are required. This is called presbyopia and affects everyone the world over, usually from about the age of forty. It is because of presbyopia that many need bifocal or varifocal glasses to see clearly at all distances. Most people deal with presbyopia by buying a simple pair of reading glasses.

Nowadays we can treat nearly all uncorrected refractive errors, or URE, by glasses or contact lenses by refocusing light so that it strikes the retina at precisely the right point. By using carefully crafted lenses to hit the retina at just that spot, people's clear vision can be simply restored.

So, although we may never have the vision of the eagle or even the box jellyfish, improvements are just around the corner for billions of people.

Long or Short – Another Conundrum

One great conundrum is why people in some parts of the world are predominantly short-sighted and in others long-sighted.

Refractive error – myopia for short-sightedness and hyperopia for long – varies markedly from one part of the world to another. More than half of all Japanese people are myopic, compared to less than 10 per cent of people in Nigeria. Europe and the United States lie somewhere between these extremes, with about a quarter of the population suffering from myopia.

Refractive error also changes over the course of our lives: most people will become more myopic (or less hyperopic) during childhood. Refractive error then tends to stabilise during adulthood followed by a shift to far-sightedness (or less short-sightedness) in old age.

So why these variations? The short answer is that no one knows for sure.

The odds on being myopic are closely linked to whether your parents are myopic or not: if you have one myopic parent, you're twice as likely to be myopic as someone who doesn't have myopic parents; if you have two myopic parents, you're three times as likely to be myopic as someone who doesn't have myopic parents.[21]

Social factors also have their place. Studies say you're more likely to be myopic if you're born to parents with higher levels of education, higher income and professional occupations.

Research suggests that children who spend more time outdoors are at lower risk of the development of myopia. The research says that it's less about the type of activity (i.e. near versus far work) and more about actually being outside in the sun.

While I'm at it, I can dismantle a few myths. Factors that have made the news as 'causes' of myopia but have since been shown to be false include reading under low lighting, prolonged use of TV and smartphone screens, and wearing glasses with your 'full', 'partial', or 'wrong' prescription.

I should add that while these things don't cause myopia, they may cause eye strain and eye discomfort.

So what are the most common causes of vision loss? Most of us know someone who suffers from cataracts.

A cataract is a clouding of the lens inside the eye (the crystalline lens) which prevents clear vision in much the same way as a very dirty window prevents one from seeing clearly through it. Cataracts develop over many years, and problems may at first be unnoticeable. They are the main cause of vision loss in people over the age of forty and are the principal cause of blindness in the world. Cataracts can be removed from the eye using a surgical procedure that takes twenty minutes to perform. A standard cataract surgery can cost as little as $20 per eye in the developing world or as much as $5,000 in the developed world.

Glaucoma is a condition that causes irreversible damage to the light-sensitive cells within the eye. Glaucoma can develop over many years, and problems may at first be unnoticeable so regular eye examinations are vital for early detection. Glaucoma is most commonly associated with high pressures within the eye and, while it is not possible to reverse existing damage, it is possible to control the advance of the condition with eye drops or, in some cases, surgery. Treatment can cost as little as $0.90 a day for eye drops or as much as $5,000 for surgery.

Trachoma is caused by a bacterial infection of the membrane that covers the eye and the inside surfaces of the eyelids. This infection is easily transmitted through contact with the tears of an infected person. Repeated infections over the years can cause the membrane on the inside surfaces of the eyelids to scar and contract, forcing the eyelashes to turn inwards and scratch the cornea. This painful condition results in blindness if not detected and treated early. If caught early, treatment with eye drops can cost as little as $1, but if scarring of the eye has occurred then surgery may cost as much as $5,000.

Macular degeneration is a painless condition that damages the light-sensitive cells in the part of the retina that is responsible for high-detail colour vision. Macular degeneration is another condition that can develop over many years and can be hard to detect. There is no cure for macular degeneration, but for certain forms of the condition there are surgical treatments that can help to slow the progression of the disease.

Diabetic retinopathy is a condition that damages the light-sensitive cells within the eye. Diabetes causes the sugar levels within the blood to fluctuate uncontrollably. If left untreated, the fine blood vessels within the eye begin to break down and leak, which damages the cells in the retina. Treatment of diabetic retinopathy may require a surgical procedure that relies on the use of lasers. This surgery may cost as much as $2,500 per eye.

So that's the eye, a fiendishly complicated organ, and the problems that can affect it. And for so many of those affected, the answer is glasses.

CHAPTER 7

THE GREAT GLASSES RUSH

The islands of Murano on the northern outskirts of Venice can with fair justification lay claim to being the birthplace of spectacles – which is why we chose this enchanted part of Italy as the venue for our Clearly event to plan the next stages of our groundbreaking campaign to help the world to see.

Given the amazing advances by human civilisation over thousands of years, it is surprising that it took until the thirteenth century for the great innovators to come up with a way to help us see better. The Roman orator Cicero complained how bothersome it was for him to have his slaves read out texts. Emperor Nero watched his beloved gladiator battles through an emerald.

In view of my heritage it would be convenient if I could assert that the first eyeglasses originated in China, and indeed some accounts of Marco Polo's travels to China claim that he saw elderly Chinese wearing eyeglasses. It does seem that Chinese judges in the twelfth century wore a type of sunglasses, made from quartz crystals, to prevent witnesses seeing the expressions on their faces. But these were sunglasses, not corrective eyewear, and the claims about Marco Polo have been debunked since those who scrutinised his notebooks have found no mention of eyeglasses.

Most historians agree that it was the creation by Johannes Gutenberg of the first printing press that led to a surge in demand for what came to be known as spectacles.

In his brilliant book *How We Got to Now*, Steven Johnson put this and other advances down to what he called the 'hummingbird effect'.[22]

He pointed out that despite the restrictions placed on them by their skeletal structure, hummingbirds evolved a novel way of rotating their wings, giving power to the up-stroke as well as the down-stroke, which enables them to float in mid-air while extracting nectar from a flower. 'These are the strange leaps that evolution makes constantly; the sexual reproduction strategies of plants ends up shaping the design of a hummingbird's wings.'

According to Johnson, the history of ideas and innovation unfolds the same way. Gutenberg's press created demand for glasses as the new practice of reading made Europeans suddenly realise they were a far-sighted lot.

So the market demand for spectacles encouraged a growing number of people to produce and experiment with lenses, which led to the invention of the microscope, which shortly afterwards enabled scientists to perceive that our bodies were made up of tiny cells.

'You wouldn't think that printing technology would have anything to do with the expansion of our vision down to the cellular scale, just as you wouldn't have thought that the evolution of pollen would alter the design of a hummingbird's wing,' Johnson writes. 'But that is the way change happens.'

But we have got ahead of ourselves. First of all, how did we get glass? Johnson puts that down to a mystery event some 26 million years ago over the sands of the Libyan desert. Grains of silica melted and fused under intense heat. They formed compounds of silicon dioxide, which has a much higher melting point than water. The peculiar thing was what happened when it cooled. It formed a new substance that existed in a strange limbo between solid and liquid. When those superheated grains of sand cooled down below melting point, a vast stretch of that desert was coated with glass.

About 10,000 years ago, someone stumbled across a frag-
ment of that glass. It ended up as the centrepiece of a brooch
carved into the shape of a scarab beetle. 'It sat there undis-
turbed for 4,000 years until it was unearthed in 1922 during
exploration of the tomb of an Egyptian ruler,' Johnson explains. 'That small sliver of silicon had found its way from
the Libyan desert to the burial chamber of Tutankhamun.'

Glass then made a dramatic transition from ornament to
advanced technology during the Roman Empire, but after
the sacking of Constantinople in 1204, a small community of
glassmakers sailed from Turkey across the Mediterranean to
Venice, where they began plying their trade in this prosper-
ous new city.

Their skills at blowing glass 'quickly created new luxury
goods for the famed merchants of Venice', says Johnson.
(Shakespeare was to tell us about one of them!) But the
practice was dangerous because their furnaces, creating
temperatures of 1,000 degrees celcius, were housed in a
city made almost entirely of wooden structures. So, in 1291,
they were exiled again – but this time only a mile across the
lagoon to the islands of Murano.

As Johnson relates, the doges of Venice had unwitting-
ly created an innovation hub on an island the size of a city
neighbourhood, and ideas were swift to flow through this
small area. Its genius was a collective affair.

By the early years of the next century, Murano had
become known as the Isle of Glass, and its exquisite glass-
ware became a status symbol throughout Western Europe.
After years of trial and error, the Murano glassmaker Angelo
Barovier took seaweed rich in potassium oxide and man-
ganese, burned it to create ash and then added it to molten

glass. When it cooled, it created an amazingly clear type of glass. He called it *cristallo*. 'It was the birth of modern glass,' writes Johnson.

As we have described elsewhere, light does not simply pass through glass. It can also be refracted. Glass, it was discovered back then, could be used to change the look of the world by bending light in precise ways.

So now, as Johnson explains, the invention of clear glass led to spectacles. 'In the monasteries of the twelfth and thirteenth centuries, monks labouring over religious manuscripts in candlelit rooms used curved chunks of glass as a reading aid. They would run these magnifiers over the page, enlarging the Latin inscriptions.'

According to a history of spectacles put together by the eye-care company Zeiss, to make the lenses, the monks used a type of quartz called beryl.[23] The history added that only a few years later – in 1267 – the Oxford Franciscan monk Roger Bacon provided scientific proof that small letters could be magnified with lenses that were ground in a specific fashion.

Somewhere around this time, the glassmakers in northern Italy came up with an innovation that would change all our lives. They shaped glass into small discs that bulged in the centre, placed each one in a frame and joined the frame at the top. 'They had created our first spectacles,' wrote Johnson.

They were called *roidi da ogli*, or 'discs for the eyes' and are illustrated at the start of this chapter. Thanks to their resemblances to lentil beans – *lentes*, in Latin – they came to be called lenses. Yes, that's how we got the word.

For a few generations, these ingenious devices belonged only to monastic scholars. Most people did not realise they suffered from presbyopia because they did not read. *Roidi da ogli* were rare and expensive objects.

But then along came Gutenberg with his printing press in the 1440s. Literacy rates rose sharply, and a massive number of people became aware for the first time that they could not see properly. Demand soared.

There was a new market for the making of spectacles. Within 100 years of Gutenberg's invention, thousands of spectacle makers across Europe were thriving, and glass became the first part of advanced technology that people would wear on their bodies. Johnson says that 'Europe was not just awash in lenses but also in ideas about lenses'. The Continent was populated with people who were experts at manipulating light through slightly convex pieces of glass. Their experiments would inaugurate a whole new chapter in the history of vision. The hummingbird effect had struck again.

By 1590, in the small town of Middelburg in the Netherlands, father and son spectacle makers Hans and Zacharias Janssen experimented with lining up two lenses, not side by side but in line with each other, magnifying the objects they observed. The microscope had arrived, to be followed by the telescope, the mirror and other familiar objects of today.

Zeiss accords the honour of the birthplace of spectacles to Murano. It points out that the glassmakers there

were the only ones who had the ability to manufacture the absolutely essential soft glass. The first quality specifications were defined a short time later. These spectacles, called reading aids, had a convex ground lens. The edge was made from iron, horn or wood. Only a single mounting style was available at the time. In general, the first spectacles were used exclusively as visual aids to enable far-sighted individuals to read.

Although it seems certain that glass from Murano was used in the first spectacles, no one is certain precisely where the first ones were invented, although most of the clues point to the Venice region.

The College of Optometrists did its own investigation and concludes that it is now generally accepted that spectacles were invented, or improvised, no later than the last quarter of the thirteenth century and that their specific area of origin centred on the Venice region, rather than Pisa or Florence, although both places still have avid supporters who back their claims. The college possesses an early printed copy of Bacon's *Opus Majus*, in which he outlined the scientific principles behind the use of corrective lenses. But no evidence survives to suggest Bacon ever applied his theoretical knowledge of optics.

The college says that in 1282 a priest named Nicholas Bullet is alleged to have used spectacles while signing an agreement. More significantly, in 1284, *De Crisalleris*, a chapter of the by-laws of the Venetian guilds, prohibited the use of ordinary white glass instead of crystal, in order to maintain high standards. And further Venetian state decrees of 1300 and 1301 refer to *roidi da ogli* as well as reading lenses. This suggests that the improvements in lens-making technology in the area of Venice was crucial to the development of spectacles.

The college concludes: 'In summary, the invention of spectacles is shrouded in mystery ... They were certainly being made and written about in Venice by 1300 at the latest and were being spoken of in Pisa (apparently retrospectively) in 1305.'

According to Zeiss:

It wasn't until around 200 years later that the first spectacles that resembled modern glasses were manufactured, when rivet spectacles were replaced by temple spectacles, with a frame consisting of one piece. Naturally, only wealthy people could afford the spectacles made from iron or bronze.

In Spain, particularly large models of spectacles were considered a status symbol. Leather nose bridges also came into use for the first time, as a way of making the visual aid more comfortable to wear. The greatest problem at that time was actually the setting. The spectacle frame would consistently slide off the nose and in many cases was so heavy that users found these spectacles rather uncomfortable to wear.

Zeiss adds:

The so-called Nuremberg rimmed spectacles appeared on the market in the eighteenth century. People gave them the not-so-flattering name of 'nose-crushers' – but they became a hit nevertheless, offering a level of wearing comfort that until then had been considered impossible.

Around the end of the eighteenth century, spectacles with a single lens called monocles became very trendy. The monocle was worn by society's dignified ladies and gentlemen in Germany and England. The French preferred the 'pince-nez' (nose-pincher) spectacles. Also spectacles with a single lens, they were not only worn on the nose, but were also sustained by the muscles around the eye. The French version had the advantage that it could be put away quickly when in the company of others because Germany's western neighbours were still embarrassed to be caught wearing their pince-nez.

The cultural barrier in Western Europe is largely overcome. One day, we hope, the same will happen in India, China and elsewhere.

The developed world has moved on a long way since then with its exquisitely fashionable, and expensive, eyewear. But what were fantastic advances back in the thirteenth century have still to reach many parts of the developing world. None of us should be proud of that.

PART III

THE
VISIONARIES

CHAPTER 8

GIANTS OF THE EYE WORLD

In Greek mythology, the giant Orion was blinded and carried his servant Cedalion on his shoulders to act as his eyes. It is said that the phrase 'standing on the shoulders of giants' derives from this story, although it was, of course, Isaac Newton who gave it its most familiar expression. In my work on poor vision, I have certainly stood on the shoulders of the giants of the eye world. The issue has largely been forgotten, yet a handful of individuals in every continent have devoted their lives to tackling it. I cannot possibly tell all their stories, but those who follow – each leading a major organisation dedicated to sight – have particularly inspired me.

Jordan Kassalow – Not a Handout but a Handshake

It was a life-changing experience for himself and a seven-year-old Mexican boy that set Jordan Kassalow on the road that led to the creation of VisionSpring, the supplier of glasses to Rwanda and many other parts of the world, and now to EYElliance, the multi-sector organisation dedicated to tackling poor eyesight in the developing world.

Jordan was twenty-three and studying optometry in Boston, Massachusetts when, on a working trip to the Yucatán Peninsula, he met the young lad, who was a student from the School for the Blind in Mexico. He was one of thousands of people who had come to the clinic where Jordan and a team of optometrists and trainees were working.

He was Jordan's first patient. The boy had his braille book with him and 'had the blank stare of a blind person'. Indeed, he was living the life of a blind person and was regarded as such by his family and community.

Jordan examined the boy and twigged that something was unusual, although he did not know what it was. He called his professor, who had a good long look and then turned to Jordan, saying, 'This boy is not blind. He has profound near-sightedness.' His prescription was so high that he could only see an inch from his nose, but he was not blind.

The team had brought 5,000 pairs of glasses with them for this programme and Jordan went to the box with the strongest prescriptions and found a pair that almost matched the young boy's needs.

> I was lucky enough to be the person that put the glasses on that boy, and as the lens aligned with his eyes, that blank stare became a smile of utter joy. He could see, probably for the first time in his life.
>
> It was a simple moment that changed his life and my life. I gave him his vision. He gave me my vision. I knew at that instant if I could go on recreating that experience I would be doing something that was worthwhile. It was an infectious moment and led me to a decision that I would define the success of my life by how often I could go on creating those moments of joy for people who just needed a pair of glasses or maybe simple treatment.

It would be another fifteen years before Jordan launched Vision-Spring, a not-for-profit body whose ambitious aim, like Clearly's, is to get glasses to all those in the world who need them.

It was another experience in South America that convinced him that glasses must not only be affordable but acceptable to the customer if his mission to help the disadvantaged was to bear fruit.

He was in Colombia when an indigenous 43-year-old Chocó Indian lady, who was known as the 'blind lady from the village', canoed down the river to a clinic that Jordan and others were running.

Like the Mexican boy, she was not blind but had a serious near-sight problem. Her reading was severely short-sighted and she also had astigmatism. Again, Jordan was able to find glasses that met her needs, and suddenly this so-called blind lady could see with near-perfect vision.

> We were proud of ourselves. Another person saved, we thought. But two days later that lady came back and sat in front of me. She told me that back in the village she had been laughed at because her glasses looked so ridiculous.
>
> And of course she was right. The only glasses we had for her were the old-fashioned, cat-eye-style, heavy-rimmed glasses, which did look very strange on her. It was a sad moment when she took those glasses off, put them on the table and went off back to her village, prepared not to see properly rather than be ostracised.
>
> I was to face opposition from my friends but this episode convinced me that we had to work on providing the right kind of glasses, we had to understand the cultural problems, that it would probably be better if people paid a small sum for the glasses rather than had them handed down to them.
>
> I thought we had to have a partnership with the customer. We had to have not a handout, but a handshake.

This experience sent Jordan on the way to starting the social enterprise that became VisionSpring, which in turn has helped tens of thousands of 'vision entrepreneurs', most of them women, to create businesses selling glasses to people who needed them to sustain their livelihoods.

VisionSpring works in partnership with bodies like the development organisation BRAC (Building Resources Across Communities) in Bangladesh and VFAN in Rwanda and helps them to use their existing distribution networks to add vision services to their product offering. VisionSpring operates this model in over a dozen countries including India, Guatemala, Haiti and Uganda.

Jordan told me that VisionSpring, which trained an army of sales agents 20,000-strong, had sold over 4 million pairs of glasses over the past fifteen years. 'But as we did that, it has become more and more apparent that if that figure was 10 million or 100 million we would still only be making a dent in this worldwide problem.'

He and Liz Smith founded EYElliance to bring a multi-sector approach – governments, NGOs, philanthropists, businesses and the eye-care community – to what he says would otherwise be an intractable problem.

As Jordan told me:

When researchers came originally to this problem, they took the Western perspective that if your vision could be corrected with glasses, you were not considered visually impaired or blind. What they failed to appreciate was that if you live in many of the developing countries and have simple refractive errors, you don't have automatic access to glasses and you might not even know you have a problem.

In its report, Eyeglasses for Global Development, using data supplied to the lens-makers Essilor by Boston Consulting

Group, EYElliance stated that the overall unmet need for vision correction affects 2.5 billion people.

Of these, 624 million need corrective lenses so strong that they are classified as visually impaired or blind without glasses, it said. But in 2015, NGOs and inclusive businesses collectively distributed fewer than 8 million pairs of eyeglasses in the countries concerned.

Jordan is a strong backer of deregulation within the eyecare industry. He, too, calls it 'task-shifting', so that jobs currently done by the professionals could be done by properly trained, albeit lower-paid, workers. 'I think the whole concept of demedicalising screening is very important. There is no reason why it should not be done by teachers in schools, for example.'

Caroline Harper – Helping the Surgeons

Caroline Harper never tires of 'the big reveal', the moment when the bandages come off the eyes after an eye operation.

At that moment, a person who might have thought wrongly that they were permanently blind sees clearly again for the first time in years and smiles in wonderment.

Recalling a recent case in which a Mozambique man, who had not been able to see for twenty-two years, had an operation and saw his grandchildren for the first time, Caroline said: 'They are the times which are the most rewarding for organisations like us. And we do a quarter of a million of them every year.'

Caroline has been chief executive of Sightsavers since 2005. Of all the organisations across the world involved in trying to tackle vision impairment, it is probably the best-known, and examples of its work are regularly seen on our television screens. It is also the biggest, spending £300 million on eye care in 2015.

It has a fantastic record, being responsible for close to 7 million sight-restoring cataract operations around the globe as well as more than 300,000 surgeries for trichiasis, caused by repeated instances of the eye infection trachoma, where scarring makes the eyelid turn inside out and grow inwards towards the eye, scraping the cornea and causing blindness.

By the end of 2016, Sightsavers had delivered more than 90 million treatments for trachoma – tackling the infection before it leads to the scarring. It has delivered nearly 390 million treatments for river blindness, a disease caused by infection by a parasitic worm, with around 47 million per year in 2015 and 2016. It trains more than 300,000 primary eye-care workers, community volunteers, specialist teachers and cataract surgeons each year. In Britain, it is usually older people who suffer from cataracts; in some developing countries, children are born with them.

Caroline is a strong backer of all moves to counter uncorrected refractive errors, the biggest cause of vision impairment, and of Clearly's mission to draw attention to the problem. She said that strengthening the primary eye-care system was 'fundamental' to the success of efforts to prevent blindness and improve access to eye health services including correction of refractive error across the world. She applauded VFAN's focus on primary eye care.

Sightsavers began life in 1950 as the British Empire Society for the Blind. Its founder, Sir John Wilson CBE, was himself blind, and his widow, Lady Jean Wilson OBE, is now ninety-three. She remains an active vice-president of the organisation, which was previously known as the Royal Commonwealth Society for the Blind.

It was after the BBC television programme *Blue Peter* launched its famous 'Sight Savers' appeal in 1987 to raise more than £2 million for eye care across Africa that the society adopted the name Sightsavers.

Sir John had swiftly noted that the international economic cost of blindness was 'astonishing', an argument pushed by the many other bodies that have emerged during the subsequent decades and is a central feature of the Clearly campaign.

One of the biggest problems with tackling visual impairment in the developing countries is the shortage of ophthalmologists and optometrists.

So, just as in Rwanda VFAN has pioneered the training of nurses to carry out vision screening, so have organisations like Sightsavers looked for ways of lightening the load of the doctors by using healthcare workers and nurses to do more of the preparatory work.

Caroline told me how in countries like Malawi and Uganda, ophthalmic nurses were being trained to carry out cataract operations, replacing the eye's crystalline lens with an intraocular lens to remove cataracts. This would be after at least a year's training. Nurses were also trained to do trichiasis surgery.

According to the *Tropical Medicine & International Health* journal, non-physician cataract surgeons work in seventeen sub-Saharan countries, including Kenya, Ghana, Zambia and Tanzania.[24]

In many countries served by Sightsavers, teachers are being asked to carry out simple eye screening tests on all the children in the school, providing lists of those who need vision correction and those who do not to save the time of the optometrist who would eventually visit the school.

In Pakistan, female health workers travel to people's houses to carry out screening tests, usually on women who spend most of their time in the home.

These are all examples of the kind of deregulation that we believe is essential if bodies like Sightsavers and Clearly are to achieve their goals.

Caroline Harper admits that one big problem is convincing the professionals that some of their jobs should be done by people with few qualifications further down the chain in order to ease their own heavy burden. 'They don't always like it,' she said. 'They say things like, "You would not want a nurse to operate on your eye." I reply that if they have had the training and experience, I would be quite OK with it.'

She added:

The problem here is scale. The work VFAN has done in Rwanda is wonderful. But how could you achieve that in countries where the governments put less of a priority on eye health and where health delivery systems are not so advanced? It is difficult. Or in much bigger countries with remote populations? How would you do in Nigeria, for example, what VFAN has done in Rwanda?

To emphasise the point, she noted that there are countries where Sightsavers has been unable to operate because of instability, most recently South Sudan.

Caroline believes the proliferation of health centres in developing-world countries will play an increasing role in finding people in surrounding villages who need glasses or treatment and then making sure they can get to a hospital if there is a referral for an operation.

> The network is huge and we have to find a way of coordinating across countries. We need to help people get to the centres and then to help them get to the clinics and hospitals if they need further treatment. There is no easy answer to this; otherwise it would have been found already.

Caroline pointed out that some countries have laws preventing the kind of deregulation that is needed. 'They insist that only doctors can perform any kind of surgical procedure. The people with the problems are likely to be in the rural areas. What professionals there are tend to be in the capital cities. That is a huge obstacle.'

It seems extraordinary to me that a regulation that has been proven obsolete in a country like Rwanda should be preventing more people being treated. Regulations are normally designed to protect people, but in the eye industry, they are all too often about protecting the professionals at the expense of ordinary people. I was delighted to hear Caroline Harper acknowledge this problem.

Brian Doolan – Grab the Low-Hanging Fruit

Brian Doolan is the man to have on your side when you are trying to break down the obstacles that have for too long stood in the way of people all over the world getting a very basic right – the right to see. Like Clearly, his is part of a community of organisations across the world fighting to address this disability. As we saw earlier, Brian is a harsh critic of the people he terms a 'medieval cabal'.

Brian is a fighter for social and economic justice. After many years working to improve the health of the Aboriginal communities, he became chief executive of the famed Fred Hollows Foundation, a development organisation now working in more than twenty-five countries that seeks to prevent and cure blindness and visual impairment among those in extreme poverty by training surgeons and other healthcare workers, funding treatments and surgeries, building and upgrading medical facilities, providing equipment, funding research and supporting advocacy.

The foundation's purpose: to make sure everyone, whether they're rich or poor, has access to high-quality, affordable eye health. To that end, the organisation works across Africa and Asia, including Rwanda, the Palestinian territories, Myanmar and Bangladesh.

It was founded in September 1992 by Fred Hollows shortly before he died. Hollows was a skilled eye surgeon committed to improving the health of indigenous Australians and to reducing the cost of eye healthcare and treatment in developing countries. He had already started work in Eritrea, Nepal and Vietnam when he died and his widow Gabi ensured that his work carried on through the foundation.

The foundation has performed over 2 million sight-restoring operations and treatments. In many cases, all it took was a twenty-minute procedure costing as little as $25.

When Brian first met Fred Hollows and they had a drink in a pub in rural Australia, he could never have imagined that twenty-five years later he would be in charge of the foundation set up in Fred's honour. Their paths crossed in the late '70s, when Brian was working in Wilcannia, in regional New South Wales, to establish an independent and indigenous-run medical and education centre. Fred Hollows was performing eye surgeries there.

Just as Clearly has made headway in Rwanda, the foundation has made huge strides forward in some countries and has shown the way ahead. As an example, Brian cites Cambodia, where the foundation works with other partners in delivering training for local doctors and eye health workers. Recently, it negotiated an agreement with the Ministry of Education to train over 12,000 teachers in recognising and referring eye health problems, developing an eye health curriculum for schools and ensuring over 600,000 children get their eyes checked. The ministry are planning to take the programme to a national level. It is a quiet revolution that is putting eye health on the agenda in Cambodia and provides a potential model for many countries. Vietnam is close to achieving ambitious targets for the treatment of trachoma, an infectious disease that causes a roughening of the inner part of the eyelids. All of this shows that what we are calling for can be implemented – with the will.

And here lies the crux of it all. When we chatted, Brian told me:

It takes about five minutes in this arena to realise that sight correction and avoidable blindness are not issues of medicine or science. The biggest issues of all are poverty and gender. Whether it be a cataract operation, medicine to treat trachoma, or just a simple pair of glasses, the big question is affordability at an individual or country level. It is estimated we would need $128 billion to tackle avoidable blindness in the developing world. Given that the total of aid for health from all sources is some $36 billion, there is no question of getting the money there.

Nearly two thirds of people living with avoidable blindness and low vision are women. Women are less likely to travel outside their villages than the men and therefore less likely to get treatment. It is often men who control the family income. There are often cultural reasons that make it difficult for a woman to be treated by another man. Communicable diseases like trachoma are transmitted through children via secretions and who is it that is more likely to be picking the children up? Yes, the woman.

So Brian believes, like us, in greater deregulation to enable more grades of health worker to screen patients, carry out eye tests and even to perform small operations. He believes in the decentralisation of eye services to regional and district level. He believes big companies with supply chains running through continents should do more by making sure the drivers of the vehicles used to carry their products are properly eye tested. 'I fear there may be drivers careering around Asia and Africa who have less than perfect eyesight,' he says.

Most of all, he believes, it is political will that is the key, making governments across the world understand that giving higher priority to eye health is a productivity issue. 'This is not about what we don't know. We have the science. We have the medicine. We have to have the political will.'

Brian says that once governments in Asia, Africa and Latin America can see how improving their nation's health can help their economies – just as Paul Kagame, the President, has in Rwanda – tackling eye health should be the 'low-hanging fruit in their priorities'. Brian adds: 'Improving people's sight is cheap, it is quick and it makes a huge impact. We have reached a position where nurses can diagnose and often all that is needed to make a huge advance in someone's life is a pair of glasses.'

Why has the world not acted before? Brian believes that one reason is that governments have traditionally seen the provision of glasses as a private-sector responsibility and have just not got to grips with absurd pricing policies.

It is pretty crazy that you can manufacture a pair of specs for $2 in China and be spending $600 on them in the United States. Some companies like Specsavers have tried to break through the pricing system but not much has happened. As for the cost of operations, the price of cataract surgery in some countries is scandalous.

When I told Brian about my plans for Clearly, he could not have been more encouraging. 'We have to create the political will to act across the world – and we can only do that if we shock the world by exposing the extent of this problem. Go for it,' he told me.

I love Brian's enthusiasm, commitment and optimism. There are many lessons for us in the work of his foundation.

FREDERICK

Acquiring glasses when you need them is a huge boost to your quality of life.

But for one man, Frederick Byumvuhore, a man whose life has been touched by the most terrible tragedy, it changed everything, and I am proud to tell his moving story.

Frederick, born in Burera in the northern province of Rwanda, is security manager at the Rwanda Trading Company in Kigali, where he has worked for over thirty years. He is responsible for all the staff there, including seasonal workers, as well as visitors, vehicles and equipment.

Reading and writing are needed for almost every aspect of his work. He has to verify ID cards at the start and end of each day, read and record licence plates, and record the weight of loads on departing company vehicles. The Clearly research team called in to see Frederick and his lovely family on their trip to Rwanda in February 2017.

He needs his job to provide for his wife Therese and their three children. It is his second family. All of his previous family, a wife and three children – a seventeen-year-old son, and daughters aged fourteen and eleven – died in the genocide against the Tutsi in Rwanda in the mid-1990s. Because of what has gone before, Frederick holds dear his life and his family. He told us that he did not want to 'dwell on the bad moments of the past'.

A few years ago, however, when Frederick was a security guard, he started to experience blurry vision, and it became harder and harder for him to read and write – two critical skills for his job.

He says: 'Writing became a terrible challenge. I could not see what I had put on paper. For reading I had to hold papers away from me in order to see.' He often asked his friends and colleagues for help.

Frederick knew in his heart that he could not perform his essential job functions any more, and was on the point of resigning.

'I thought that my life was over,' he told the Clearly visitors. 'I use reading and writing in my job. If I did not have glasses my life would have stopped.'

He knew that glasses were the solution but he was unable to afford them. All the money he earnt was spent on his family.

Then came a good piece of news for this man who had re-built his life after the horrors of the 1990s.

As he was preparing to stand down from work, he heard that a team from Vision for a Nation and the Rwandan Ministry of Health were visiting his company to conduct eye assessments. 'I knew it was the answer,' he says.

And it was. Within days, a trained nurse had given Frederick an eye test and confirmed he was a candidate for reading glasses, which he swiftly obtained.

He knew that his job had been saved and that he could go on providing for his second, loving family. Now he has no difficulty reading and writing. 'I no longer need to ask someone to help with my reading. I am so thankful.'

The impact on Frederick's life was amazing. Instead of losing his job, he retained it and two months later he was promoted to be head of all security for his company. At home, he has become a village leader, trying to encourage his neighbours to do what he did and get their eyes examined. 'With those glasses I can do anything. But whether at work or at home, without them I cannot do anything.'

He added:

If you went with me to the office, you would see my glasses there on the table, just as you can see them here at home in this room. When a neighbour has a problem, I put on my glasses and help him or her. I wear them for any kind of reading or writing.

He also hopes he can provide for his children in the future and to help them pursue their dreams. Devalier, his eldest, is in the final year of secondary school and wants to be a mechanical engineer. Gabril, seven, likes drawing and painting and shows promise to be an artist or designer. Violet, four, is an early reader who loves books and writing.

Frederick says: 'I hope little by little, day by day, we will improve our lives and my children can achieve their dreams.'

Understandably, Frederick becomes grave when talking about the past.

You have to have patience and hope because they make life continue. When you hold on to hope and patience you are not alone. You have people around you. You don't get lost in bad thoughts. When my vision started failing, I received the help I needed in the form of glasses. Those glasses helped me have hope for my future life. Having hope means not holding on to problems and remembering

Felicien Senzoga putting the finishing touches to a garment in his
Kigali textile factory. © Sarah Day Smith/VFAN.

Felicien keeps his prescription for his reading glasses in his wallet just in case he loses them.
© Sarah Day Smith/VFAN.

Felicien helping his daughters with their homework on his Sunday rest day.
© Sarah Day Smith/Clearly.

Augustin Ngarambe has just had his eyes examined at a village in Rwanda. A nurse tells him that he will be referred to the local hospital. © Sarah Day Smith/Clearly.

Augustin, a builder until his eyes started troubling him, walked for miles to have his vision tested at the Zinga outreach. © Sarah Day Smith/Clearly.

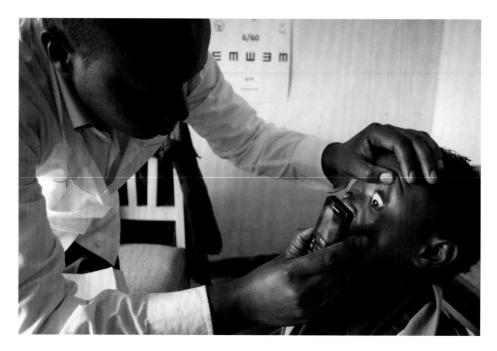

Regine Mukasine having her eyes tested at Mukono health centre in Rwanda.
© Sarah Day Smith/VFAN.

Pascal Masengesho, a nurse trained to conduct vision screening and dispense glasses,
examined Regine and prescribed her glasses. © Sarah Day Smith/VFAN.

Regine with the notebook she used to prepare for her exams. Receiving glasses gave her a second chance to work towards her dream of going to nursing school. © Sarah Day Smith/VFAN.

Maria Nyiranzayire with her new pair of adjustable glasses which she said had made her a happier person. © Sarah Day Smith/Clearly.

Patients waiting to be seen at the vision centre at Rwamagana Hospital in the eastern province of Rwanda. © Sarah Day Smith/Clearly.

Rwamagana Hospital in the eastern province of Rwanda has its own ophthalmology department. It serves sixteen health centres. © Sarah Day Smith/Clearly.

Sam Ndihakaniye worked as an electrician with the Rwandan Army before working on a cooperative farm with his friends. © Sarah Day Smith/Clearly.

A woman smiles as she sees clearly for the first time in years while having her eyes tested at the Zinga outreach. © Sarah Day Smith/Clearly.

Theophille Ingabire reading the announcements in her local church in Kabuye, Rwanda. Without her glasses that would have been impossible. © Sarah Day Smith/Clearly.

Theophille, who works as a tailor in Kigali, reading her Bible at home with the glasses prescribed under the Vision for a Nation scheme. © Sarah Day Smith/Clearly.

your people whom you lost in the genocide. But instead you get hope and don't remain sad about those who passed away during the genocide. Hope helped me then. The fact that I got those glasses restored my hope and helped me. I was hopeless and felt I was going to die blind. God helped me and people gave me glasses.

Those glasses saved me from misery. I am here right now because of those glasses. They helped me improve my reading and writing and my neighbours voted for me to be village leader. They could not vote for me without me being able to read and write. But because of the glasses I had the trust in myself to do what they wanted me to do. Glasses help life to continue.

Frederick thanks God every day for his family, and he does not take them for granted. 'It is God who gave us life,' Frederick says. 'Everyone must die, and we each only live until it is our time... Life is like that, so we must give thanks for all we have.'

Frederick, a man who has fought back from the terrors of the 1990s, can now happily live with his world after all that he has endured; another life that has been changed completely by the simple provision of glasses.

CHAPTER 9

THE INVENTORS

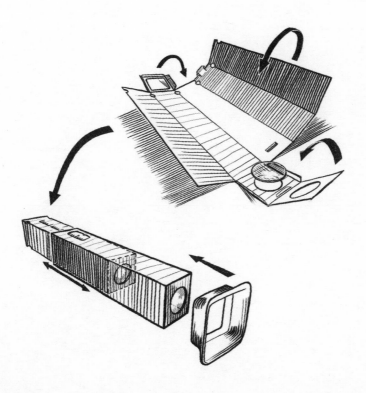

Given the prevalence of poor vision, the costs of helping the whole world see might seem to be beyond our reach. Thankfully, the ever-industrious human species continues to develop new inventions that are bringing down the cost of dealing with poor vision. No solution to this global problem would be sustainable without the kinds of innovation I have seen on my travels around the world and encouraged through the Clearly Vision Prize, which I funded in 2016. Here I tell the stories of five of the most exciting technological developments.

Dr Andrew Bastawrous – iPhone Joins Vision Battle

Dr Andrew Bastawrous, an eye surgeon, was walking towards a latrine at a rural eye clinic in Kenya when something happened that was to change his life and – one day, we hope – the lives of millions of others.

In this remote part of the Great Rift Valley, Andrew heard the sound of a mobile phone – a classic Nokia ringtone.

When Andrew, his wife and son moved to Kenya, they took with them some £100,000 of expensive diagnostic and other eye-care equipment. Andrew, who was born in the UK to Egyptian parents and schooled in Yorkshire, had gone there because he wanted to give something back to people less privileged than himself.

The figures that preyed on his mind were these: of the 36 million people in the world who are blind, 80 per cent are suffering from conditions that could be treated or cured. In other words, they are needlessly blind.

The same is true of the vast majority of the other 2.5 billion people who suffer from simple eye refraction problems. Most of them could see perfectly well if they had glasses.

Andrew was stunned when he heard the phone. Here he was in an inaccessible village with no running water or electricity. Getting here had been a trial. The roads were bad. At times, he and his team had had to get out of their van carrying the heavy equipment and push it. But mobile phones worked here.

For Andrew, who had by now begun establishing some 100 temporary clinics in the valley, it was a thunderbolt. It was this kind of village where most blind people were found; because it was so hard to get to, many never got to see a doctor, let alone an eye specialist. Surely the connectivity of a mobile phone could help. He found that while 80 per cent of the people of Kenya had access to mobile phones, only 50 per cent had running water and basic sanitation.

It was the moment that led Andrew to establish his renowned foundation and company, Peek Vision. Peek was initially named for an acronym: portable eye examination kit. And that was what it was – a simple kit replacing all that heavy-duty material that he was lugging round the villages of Kenya.

Working at the International Centre for Eye Health at the London School of Hygiene and Tropical Medicine, Andrew and his colleagues invented Peek Acuity, the app used to test eyesight easily and affordably using a smartphone as accurately as any traditional tests. And, most important, it could be done by just about anyone, certainly any health worker, with knowledge of how to use a mobile.

'Our ultimate hope is that the accuracy and easy-to-use features of Peek will lead to more people receiving timely and appropriate treatment and be given the chance to see clearly again,' he says.

Peek consists of a series of apps, a unique piece of hardware called Peek Retina and systems that connect the data from these apps to service providers, patients and key people who influence the uptake of treatment.

Andrew had realised by now that he needed to go further than his original discovery. Once his team have found that somebody has low vision, the next big challenge is to work out why, and to be able to do that, they need to have access to the inside of the eye. Traditionally, this requires expensive equipment to photograph the retina or low-cost tools such as ophthalmoscopes. The retina has huge amounts of information about the body and its health.

So they prototyped a 3D-printed, low-cost piece of hardware that can then be clipped onto a smartphone and makes it possible to get very high-quality views of the back of the eye. 'And the beauty is, anybody can do it. In our trials on over 2,500 study participants, the smartphone with the add-on clip was comparable to a desktop retinal camera that is hugely more expensive and far more difficult to transport.'

So that is Peek Retina, an empowering tool for health workers.

It was a breakthrough. Says Andrew:

We set about replacing traditional hospital equipment, which is bulky, expensive and fragile, with smartphone apps and hardware that make it possible to test anyone in any language and of any age.

We've got many trials going on in the community and in schools, and through the lessons that we've learned in the field, we've realised it's extremely important to share the data in non-medical jargon so that people understand what we're examining and what that means to them.

So here, for example, we use our PeekSim application, once your vision has been measured, to show carers and teachers what the visual world is like for that person, so they can empathise with them and help them.

Andrew continues:

When we first moved to Kenya, we went with $150,000 of equipment, a team of fifteen people, and that was what was needed to deliver healthcare. Now, all that's needed is a single person on a bike with a smartphone – and at a fraction of the cost.

The issue of power supply is overcome by harnessing the power of solar energy. Our healthcare workers travel with a solar-powered rucksack which keeps the phone charged and backed up.

Important though the development of Peek Retina is, Andrew puts even greater store on his company's pioneering of screening programmes, which in turn, he believes, will lead to more of the people suffering eye problems being treated. So the programmes, in schools, in different communities, and across populations, are designed to compile the data through entering it on an app that will allow health authorities and experts to know where the problems are.

They start with an analysis of the situation on the ground, including the numbers of professionals available, and then work from there with partners such as health ministries and NGOs to provide treatment.

He gives as an example the Kenyan Trans-Nzoia County, which borders Uganda and is a region with very few eye-care providers (and only one ophthalmologist) covering a population of 2.6 million people.

Peek's first trial of the school screening system was run here, working with teachers and eye-care workers to see if the system improved access to eye-care services. In the trial, 21,000 children were screened by twenty-five teachers in just nine days. Nine hundred children were identified with vision problems. Subsequently, the trial has evolved into a programme which will reach all school children (over 300,000) in the county but also provide supervision after treatment.

Early in 2017, more than 800 children were fitted with glasses to correct their vision thanks to the Peek Botswana school screening programme.

During the project, a total of 12,877 children had their eyes tested at forty-nine schools with Peek school screening apps and software.

For Andrew, treatment is all, and huge amounts of diagnostic work is only worthwhile if it leads to good treatment.

The old idea of health professionals spending the day at a school, only to find that, say, one in fifteen of the children needed treatment of any kind, was not a good use of their time.

Far better to let the teachers do the screening and supply the information via phone and laptop back to the authorities.

Something Andrew once said has always stuck with me: 'It's only in statistics that people go blind by the millions. The reality is everyone goes blind on their own. But now, they might just be a text message away from help.'

William Mapham – Connecting Nurses to Specialists

I launched the Clearly Vision Prize in the hope that it would throw up ideas to give me speedy assistance in my mission to help the world to see. William Mapham, a South African doctor, duly obliged and took the honours with a revolutionary app that connects primary healthcare workers in remote areas with on-call specialists around the country and – eventually, I hope – in other countries.

The Vula Mobile app, which William invented, allows trained health staff to take and share initial results and scans with on-call specialists, who are then able to offer diagnostic treatment advice for eye problems and now other conditions, across borders, and from many miles away. This is the kind of innovation we need. Remember our 4Ds. This helps us overcome the diagnosis barrier by bringing busy experts to the villages over the internet.

Thousands have been helped. People like 72-year-old Ndawayipheli and his wife Nojongile, sixty-eight, who live in Kotyana, a beautiful village over 1,300 kilometres from Cape Town. The village is surrounded by rolling green hills and its inhabitants live in brightly coloured thatched huts dotted along the lush green landscape. However, until recently, neither Ndawayipheli nor Nojongile, could enjoy the breathtaking views because both were blind. Theirs is a wonderful story that appears later in this chapter.

In deciding that Vula Mobile should take the prize of $100,000, the judges agreed that this was a project that was already up and running and could only benefit from further investment.

So, a scheme that started in the Western Cape and moved to the Eastern Cape may in the coming months and years go international. That is their hope and mine as they develop.

Vula gives health workers in rural areas the tools they need to capture accurate clinical information, guiding them through simple tests for visual acuity, finger counting, hand movements and light perception. Expert advice can be given almost instantly, especially in emergencies. The health workers complete the questionnaire, not the patients.

Patients can fill in a short medical history – the questions were decided upon in conjunction with consultants – and send snapshots. Primary healthcare workers can act as a middleman to quickly assess what kind of specialist care the patient needs. It began as a tool purely for eye care, but there are now sections for cardiology, orthopaedics, burns, HIV and dermatology. It is truly amazing.

It was while working at the Vula Emehlo eye clinic in rural Swaziland that William conceived the idea for the app.

Vula Emehlo means 'open your eyes' in a number of African languages, including Siswati and Zulu. William experienced at first hand the difficulties faced by rural health workers when they need specialist advice.

Let me tell you about William. He was born in Johannesburg to a mother of English descent and a father, a university lecturer, whose family came from the Eastern Cape. During William's third year at medical school, one of the professors announced on a ward round that nothing good comes out of the Eastern Cape. It really hit a nerve and the young man determined to prove him wrong in whatever way he could.

He had gone to St Peter's prep school in Johannesburg and grew up in a suburb near Alexandria township. It was when tear gas wafted over one day that his parents decided to look for employment overseas. With William and their three other children, they moved to a village near Newbury in leafy Berkshire and found William a place at Wellington College at nearby Crowthorne.

It was in his first year at Wellington that William decided that he wanted to be a doctor. He told me:

> My brother is partially deaf, he was being teased at school about his hearing aids and I thought I could do something about it. Wellington offered a careers guidance service. Every single aptitude test said that medicine was the last thing I should do. They did their best to push me towards marketing or a more creative industry.

William turned down a place at Edinburgh medical school to return to South Africa.

Back there, he had missed the deadline for applying to medical school and ended up working on a farm for a time. Eventually, he got into the medical school at the University of Cape Town and after that carried through his wish to work in rural hospitals. With friends, he went to live in Bulungula, where the nearest hospital was Madwaleni.

His interest in eye care was fired when he happened upon a cataract operation after wandering into the wrong theatre during an internship at Kalafong Hospital. 'I stayed for the operation and can still picture it now. It amazed me. At Madwaleni, I organised for a professor to come and specially see patients on an Eye Day. This was the start.'

On leaving Madwaleni, he visited the inspirational Dr Jono Pons in Swaziland, who ran the eye service for the country. William had a passion to do a cataract operation. Dr Jono agreed to train him as long as he didn't expect a salary. 'We predicted three months. As a slow learner, it took me ten,' he says.

Now, apart from his Vula work, William is a registrar at the ophthalmology department of Tygerberg Hospital in Cape Town.

Early in 2015, William took six months' unpaid leave from the hospital to set up Vula. The future looked tricky until Vula was selected as a finalist for the first African entrepreneurship award in Morocco. After a week of pitching their cases, Vula was one of the six winners and received $150,000. It was a lifeline.

The first award enabled William to take on Debré Barrett, a former journalist with a long-standing interest in healthcare innovation, who turned what he admits was a rudimentary system into an elegant app. She is the only full-time employee, with William and two others working part-time.

Over the months and years, the app has been developed. The health worker needs to have a mobile phone at their disposal and know-how to install the app. Doctors can take advantage of the 3D printer devices, which can now be attached to the phone, and take pictures of a patient's retina. They can screen patients for diabetes and view the optic nerve.

While Vula is available on the Apple and Android stores and anyone can download it onto their smartphone, only registered health workers are allowed to make referrals to specialists.

Debré speaks of growing interest in the app from all areas of South Africa and now from outside, including Zambia, Brazil, the Caribbean and India. 'This is an app without borders. There is no real logistical reason why a patient in one country cannot be connected to a specialist in another,' she said.

William commented:

In almost every industry, innovation in mobile solutions has offered groundbreaking progress in the fight against outdated and ineffective systems. Medicine is an industry crying out for change as it seeks to save lives and improve the health conditions of billions. Vula is just one of many health apps that are making a difference.

Vula is driven by the belief that many millions of blind people in the world could have been spared their disability had a problem such as a cataract been spotted at an earlier stage by a simple eye test, and by the knowledge that billions of others could have their lives improved by acquiring glasses.

Vula has a built-in data security system whereby patient data is deleted from phones after the referral has taken place. The data is then stored on a secure server that can be accessed later if required. Even so, the company employs the services of a lawyer to make sure that confidentiality is observed. As Dylan Edwards has remarked, the main competitor for Vula Mobile is a combination of pen, paper and fax machine, which is still the way that most medical referrals are made in low-income settings.

The way it works is this. Imagine someone in a rural village believes they have a serious eye problem. They go to the nearest clinic. When seeing a new patient, a health worker will capture their basic details in a short, simple form. The app will guide them through performing an eye test and automatically assign a visual acuity score.

Once the doctor has saved the patient's details, he or she can tap on the 'refer' button, which will bring up a list of the specialists at the hospital where they refer their eye health patients. They will be able to see which doctor is on call. Once they tap on the specialist's name, they will be able to exchange text messages with that specialist. This allows the healthcare worker to ask clinical questions and allows the specialist to find out more about the patient in real time. Together, they can then decide what the best course of care for the patient is. The specialists can review a patient's information, including test results and photographs, before the patient arrives at the referral hospital. This means doctors can prioritise urgent cases and prepare for their arrival ahead of time.

So let's go back to Ndawayipheli and Nojongile, whose story was told on the BBC website late in 2015. Both lost their sight because of cataracts – a condition that can be corrected with a twenty-minute routine surgery, but for them diagnosis and treatment is difficult to access because of the remoteness of their location. Kotyana is four hours away from Mthatha, where cataract surgery is offered, and the waiting list there is up to a year long. Recently, however, a cataract surgery service has been created less than an hour from Kotyana – which is where Nojongile was treated last year and where Ndawayipheli has since been treated.

As a result of her cataract surgery in both eyes, Nojongile can now see again and perform her daily chores. Until recently, she had to ask for help from other women in the village. She now relishes tasks such as cooking food on her open fire, and throwing stones at the birds of prey eyeing up her baby chicks.

She says:

After the operation, my eye was covered for two days. On the third day I removed the patch and I could see!

My life is so much better now. It was really bad when I was blind, I was even afraid to do a simple thing such as walking. I was afraid of hurting myself because I couldn't see where I was going.

Nojongile is no longer afraid of hurting herself, but her 72-year-old husband Ndawayipheli had to be persuaded, because he was reluctant to go under the knife.

But William visited the village to examine him using the Vula App. It means the family can also see the cataracts, which are seen more easily on a photo than in real life.

They helped to persuade Ndawayipheli to have the procedure, which took place at the very remote Zithulele Hospital.

So there we have it – Vula Mobile, opening people's eyes in a way that would not have been possible a few years ago.

Michael Young – Helping Chinese Children to See

Only about one in seven of the children who need glasses in rural and migrant areas in China actually have them, a survey by Stanford University and the country's Rural Education Action Program, has found.[25]

So it was particularly pleasing that another honour in our vision prize went to SmartFocus, a high-growth healthcare social enterprise with offices at Stanford and in China that provides low-cost eye exams and eyeglasses to millions in China, with a focus on rural, school-age and underserved populations. Michael Young, the enterprise's chief executive officer, took the award.

There are 30 million primary school children in rural China who cannot see properly because they don't have glasses. If you include middle-school children, the tally leaps to 50 million – all suffering from easily correctable vision loss.[26]

The study showed that eyeglasses not only improve the welfare of children, but also lead to extraordinary gains in school performance. As education is increasingly critical to succeed in Chinese society, correcting myopia plays a key role in extending opportunity to China's rural youth, a vast and struggling segment of China's population, says SmartFocus.

Rural China's vision crisis originates from low awareness of the need for vision care, lack of access to care, and economic challenges. Market forces alone cannot solve the crisis. What can is a scalable business model.

As Scott Rozelle, Stanford senior fellow, said: 'Based on my twenty-five years of research experience, correcting

vision with glasses is the single most effective health intervention when it comes to improving academic performance.'

The Stanford Rural Education Action Program website
said:

> Today only 16 per cent of near-sighted children have glass-
> es, making uncorrected vision the single largest paediatric
> health problem in China.
>
> Like nearly all rural children in China, near-sighted
> youngsters lag more than two years behind in academic
> achievement compared to their urban peers. This per-
> sistent achievement gap has implications for China's
> continued economic growth, as vast numbers of rural
> youth grow up unprepared to compete in the labour
> market of an increasingly modern economy.
>
> Yet one simple action – placing eyeglasses on a near-
> sighted child's face – can erase as much as half of this
> achievement gap over the course of only one academic year.

So SmartFocus is improving the vision of the next generation. It is uniting the powers of industry, government, hospitals and schools to provide high-quality, low-cost eye exams
that bring eye care directly into schools to make sure that students get the treatment they need. It focuses on young people
in rural areas who might otherwise be left behind.

People like Siyu Di, who is in grade six and wrote to the
clinic 'with a grateful heart' thanking it for the provision of
glasses.

Or Siyao Sun, from grade four, who thanked her school.

She wrote:

In order to protect my vision, improve my grades, and enhance my future studies, I will make good use of my glasses, which allow me to see better and avoid typos when I write. Thank you for supplying us rural children with glasses for free, so that we can see clearly when we put them on. I will make good use of them and study hard so that I can contribute to society in the future. At the same time, I hope that this kind of lovely event can help more students who require such assistance.

Heart-warming words from children who benefited. We must get glasses to them all.

Ashish Jain – Eye Testing with the Folding Phoropter

Origami is the art of paper folding, which has its roots in Japan.

It was used to develop the Folding Phoropter, which is illustrated at the start of this chapter and took the second prize of $50,000 in our vision prize. It is a device that I expect to play a prominent role in our fight to bring good vision to the people of the developing world. It is brilliant.

The phoropter, otherwise known as a refractor, is used to assess various lenses during the regular eye test with which most of us are familiar. The folding version was created specifically to help diagnose refractive errors quickly and cheaply in the poorer areas of the world. It is a 'telescopic' phoropter. It allows the user to compare a variety of lens powers to one another and pick whichever is best.

Lenses are placed in their designated positions in what is folded to look like a telescope, with an inner and outer part.

The patient needs to look through the device a fixed distance away from the designated target, and move the outer chamber inwards until the image just comes into focus.

It is a simple device. But using its data-driven approach, the Folding Phoropter has calibrated it on the most commonly observed refractive error ranges. It is easy to understand and intuitive to use.

The device is also extremely easy to assemble and it can be put together in a matter of minutes without prior training. Only simple origami is needed, similar to folding a parcel box or an envelope.

This radical but straightforward idea originated at Hyderabad in India. Created by the Srujana Centre for Innovation at L. V. Prasad Eye Institute, a device costs less than $0.50.

The phoropter is a simple, open-source and disposable instrument. It can accurately test for refractive error in even the most remote locations.

The device – similar to a traditional ophthalmologist's tool used to screen for refractive errors like short- or long-sightedness – was inspired by Google Cardboard, a virtual reality platform mounted round a smartphone and using folded cardboard as the viewer. It was created specifically to help diagnose the errors quickly and cheaply in low-resource areas. Ashish Jain, who – along with the institute's team of optometrists, vision scientists and engineers – designed the phoropter, took the award.

A disproportionate number of the people with visual impairment reside in rural, low-income communities, which the Folding Phoropter is targeting. The reimagined phoropter uses the most common refractive error ranges – so it won't be able to catch every error in detail. A test of the device on 100 people showed a 'strong correlation' between its readings and those taken in a clinical setting with the usual ophthalmologist tools. Like two other winners I mention later, Essmart and Maza, the phoropter will be of huge value as we advance.

Come Fly with Me – Be an Eye Surgeon

In the old days, aircraft pilots used to train by trial and error. When they took to the air on their own, with what sometimes turned out to be insufficient training, it would often have disastrous results. The world lost a lot of pilots that way.

Then along came aviation simulators, which allowed pilots to learn to fly – as well as being confronted with the occasional emergencies they would experience in the air – while sitting safely in offices on the ground.

Now, the high technology and instructional techniques that brought safety to aviation will be used to train health technicians to conduct operations to tackle the single most avoidable form of blindness on this earth: untreated cataracts.

And it is no coincidence – as we will see – that the people who worked so hard to make flying safer are behind the efforts to bring relief across the world to the avoidably blind.

Simulators have been developed to recreate the human eye in all its visual and tactile details and, used in conjunction with sophisticated technical kit, provide an endless supply of virtual eyes and unlimited opportunities for practice without endangering patients.

Just as you would not now want a pilot to take the controls without months and years of training, you would not really want a surgeon to conduct an eye operation without having been trained at length and having faced all the unexpected situations they might encounter during an operation. People going for treatment need to feel utterly confident as they put their eyes, and lives, in the hand of their surgeon.

Just as my mission is to help the billions whose lives could be changed by the provision of a simple pair of spectacles, the mission of my friend Jacob Mohan Thazhathu is to train the experts who could help the world eliminate avoidable cataract blindness.

Jacob, who took one of the innovation honours at the Clearly Vision Prize event, is the chief executive of HelpMe-See, whose crusade is to make the miracle of sight possible for every blind child and adult in the world regardless of where they live or how poorly served they may be. The first step is to eliminate cataract blindness by restoring eyesight for millions with a high-quality, simple and inexpensive surgery.

Jacob believes that only disruptive approaches – approaches that he admits would be regarded with huge suspicion by the ophthalmology establishment in the developed world – will help to solve this problem, and he told me of his dramatic goal to train 30,000 cataract surgeons over a period of ten to twelve years. Thousands of them will be people who have not gone through the long period of training required of surgeons in the developed world. He told me that under his scheme it should be possible to train a competent health professional to do the job in four months. 'The ophthalmology business interests will kill us for this,' he jokes.

He admits that it will be down to the governments in the countries he is trying to help to allow this to happen, but he is confident that they will. It is the kind of deregulation that we need across all aspects of this problem if we are to crack it. It helped me in Rwanda when nurses were allowed to conduct eye tests after just three days' training. As he says: 'In some countries, there are next to no ophthalmologists at all. Unless we train them, people have no prospect of being treated. We cannot sit and wait for the world to wake up to this. If the ophthalmologists are not there, we must put them there.' He reveals that in the Gambia, where there are a tiny number of surgeons, highly skilled nurses will be allowed to train to do operations.

Jacob and his company are revolutionaries and the world must back them.

Jacob points out that ophthalmic surgeons need two critical skills: a steady hand, including good hand–eye coordination, and depth perception to figure out how to handle the tissues that keep forming and reforming when an eye surgery is being performed. These two skills have previously been acquired only by a process of trial and error on live patients, he said.

By bringing in simulator-based training, the skillsets of the surgeons are greatly enhanced and the potential costs in terms of damaging the patient inadvertently and then facing legal suits are significantly reduced.

The simulator will enhance a surgeon's ability to achieve a higher level of proficiency before completing the live surgery that is part of training. It records and monitors surgical performance. It means a trainee can repeat individual steps of the surgery until the desired level of proficiency is achieved.

The cataract specialist's proficiency level is documented through each stage of training.

But because the training is so concentrated, the simulator should reduce the time required to acquire surgical skills and qualify for independent surgery. Once completed, simulation-based training will prove to be a more effective method to train the large numbers of qualified surgeons that are needed.

The highly advanced simulation can provide surgical training for some 250 types of errors, complications and challenges that surgeons may face in the operating room during live cataract surgery. The simulator design provides for a virtually limitless number of 'eyes' for training, with unparalleled visual realism and tactile feel.

The HelpMeSee campaign had its beginnings in the late 1970s. It was then that Albert L. Ueltschi, who is widely seen as the father of modern aviation training, dedicated himself to fighting blindness in the developing world. He was convinced that training of local providers so they could serve their communities was the answer.

As founder and leader of FlightSafety International, the world's foremost aviation training company, he thought that he had the skills and dedication to make a difference.

Al co-founded and led Orbis International for thirty years. It is best known for its 'Flying Eye Hospital'. He led the effort to outfit the original McDonnell Douglas DC-8 airplane and later its successor the DC-10 wide-body jet with surgical equipment and training rooms. For the first time, volunteer ophthalmologists could reach out to all corners of the globe to treat avoidable blindness of all types and to strengthen eye-care practices in developing countries through training.

The DC-8 became a fully functional, teaching eye hospital. Staffed by a highly skilled team of ophthalmologists, anaesthetists, nurses and biomedical technicians, the Flying Eye Hospital took off from Houston in the spring of 1982 for its first programme in Panama.

It wasn't long into the new millennium when Al began investigating the possible use of high-fidelity simulation technology to train highly skilled cataract specialists to solve the problem of cataract treatment access. With Jacob on board, Al and his son, Jim Ueltschi, brought together a team with the best talents in simulation technology, training and ophthalmology to accomplish this goal.

So it was Al (with his son Jim) who co-founded HelpMeSee with a singular purpose: to eliminate cataract blindness, bringing with him half a century's experience in simulation-based aviation training.

Al died in October 2012, but not before signing the Giving Pledge along with Bill Gates and Warren Buffett. The Al Ueltschi Foundation and the James T. Ueltschi Foundation collectively contributed the start-up cost to successfully launch the HelpMeSee campaign.

Now Jacob and his brilliant HelpMeSee team are carrying on that work. And I say hats off to them!

CHAPTER 10

A VISION
FOR RWANDA

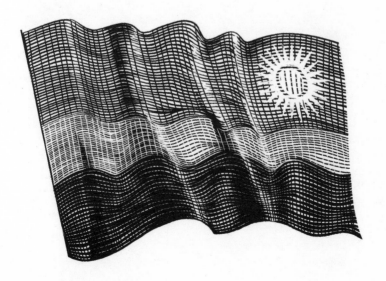

Sitting unobtrusively in KG599 Street in the Gasabo district of Kigali is a smart, gated house surrounded by trees and a pleasant garden.

It is in one of the quieter areas of this bustling capital of Rwanda and the home of Vision for a Nation, the charity I established five years ago with the unique aim of providing universal access to eye care and affordable glasses. We have pioneered a partnership with the national government to overcome big logistical challenges and deliver primary eye care to 2 million Rwandans – a sixth of the population – by the end of July 2017.

It is, as usual, a busy Monday morning as the staff here race to reach our goal of providing vision screening to all of the country's 15,000 villages by the end of 2017.

The Clearly research team has come to visit. Mondays are 'data review and field preparation day'. With country director Abdallah Uwihoreye orchestrating, the data specialists Pascal Umugwaneza and Chance Pascal are out on the terrace with the whole staff, reviewing with a large projector the screening performance results from all 502 health centres across the nation.

The 'data dudes', as the Pascals are affectionately called by outgoing boss Tom Rosewall, help us discover which centres are 'on track' to help us reach our goal and which are not.

This will enable the VFAN teams to plan their movements for the next four days – focusing primarily on visiting health centres that are not performing and getting them back on the right road.

You have to remember that the health centres – the administrators and nurses who are ultimately responsible for visiting each village in their catchment area – are the ones actually doing the work. They don't work for VFAN, and are not on VFAN's payroll. They work for the Ministry of Health. Our job is to nudge gently, and Monday morning is all about planning the nudging.

And it works!

On the face of it, Rwanda was one of the most unlikely places in the world to choose for the trailblazing work of VFAN.

The country's relatively recent history is written in blood. The shadow of the government-sponsored genocide of the mid-1990s hangs over it. Those who survived can never forget it. Neither will the world.

In one of the worst horrors since the Second World War, almost 1 million ethnic Tutsis and moderate Hutus were killed by dominant Hutu forces in 100 days. Four hundred lives of men, women and children lost for every hour of the genocide.

The so-called Land of One Thousand Hills has fought back from those terrible times. Rwanda, a landlocked nation of 12 million people, is striving to rebuild its economy, with coffee and tea production among its main exports. The World Bank has praised Rwanda's recent 'remarkable development successes', which it says have helped reduce poverty and inequality.

Paul Kagame has run Rwanda since his rebel army ended the slaughter in 1994. A 2007 statement by the President about his 'vision' for his country is emblazoned on one of the walls in the VFAN headquarters.

He was sworn in as Vice-President and Defence Minister in the new, post-genocide government in July 1994, but was widely seen as the real power in Rwanda.

In the year 2000, the Parliament elected him President. He won presidential elections in 2003 and again in 2010 and has been granted power in a referendum to stand again next year.

He has been praised by, among others, Bill Clinton and Tony Blair for the way he has presided over Rwanda's recovery. But he has also been criticised for wielding despotic powers and trampling on freedoms.

A report by Amnesty International in 2015 said that freedoms of expression and association in Rwanda continued to be unduly restricted by the authorities.[27] Rwandans were unable to openly express critical views on issues perceived as sensitive by the authorities, and the environment for journalists, human rights defenders and members of the opposition remained repressive. There were reports of unlawful detention by Rwandan military intelligence, and past cases of torture were not investigated.

However, as reported by *The Economist* in March 2017, Rwanda has made huge advances in the past two decades. The latest UN Human Development Index takes a broader look at progress, examining life expectancy and education as well as income.[28] Rwanda made the greatest strides in human development from 1990 to 2015: people there can expect to live for a staggering thirty-one years longer than in 1990, and spend twice as much time at school.

There was a downside. The UN also calculates an adjusted index that measures how much development is foregone as a result of inequality. On average, this reduces countries' 2015 scores by 22 per cent; Rwanda's fell by over 30 per cent.

It was the country's growing reputation for competent governance, as well as its established health infrastructure and relative ease of travel to most parts of the country from the capital Kigali, that convinced my close colleagues and me that it was the right place to try. We were massively helped by the fact that the Ministry of Health already had in place a network connecting Kigali with all hospitals and then on to the health centres. This was here before we arrived and without it we would have been in serious trouble. Indeed, our achievements may not have been possible.

By 2007, I had overseen the development of adjustable glasses at Adlens and formed a non-profit subsidiary to sell our products into the development aid sector. We found it impossible to interest funders like the World Bank and existing charities in the vision care sector. Out of exasperation and frustration, Vision for a Nation, a UK registered charity was formed so that we could try to do what the development aid sector and the professional community said could not be done. My one journey on vision at this point became two parallel journeys for me: one the development of the adjustable power lens technology as a for-profit (sustainable) enterprise and the other a not-for-profit charitable enterprise focused on finding answers to the issue of access to vision correction in unserved or underserved communities.

Vision for a Nation works by training the ministry's existing workforce of general nurses to provide vision assessments and dispense glasses to all who need them. The nurses sell low-cost reading glasses and cutting-edge adjustable glasses that instantly change focus at the turn of a dial for 1,000 francs ($1.50), equivalent to five days' disposable income for the average Rwandan, and free to those classified by government as very poor.

Rwanda had set itself the ambitious task of attaining middle-income country status by the year 2020 through

Asha Abubakar travelled to Zanzibar for treatment for her blinding cataracts. Here she is being examined. © Sightsavers/Tommy Trenchard.

Happy Asha after her operation at Kibweni Hospital in Zanzibar. © Sightsavers/Tommy Trenchard.

Sackey Vaness was prescribed glasses through a Sightsavers programme in Ghana. They helped him with his school work. The programme was run in partnership with the World Bank, Imperial College London's Partnership for Child Development and the Global Partnership for Education. © Sightsavers/Ruth McDowall.

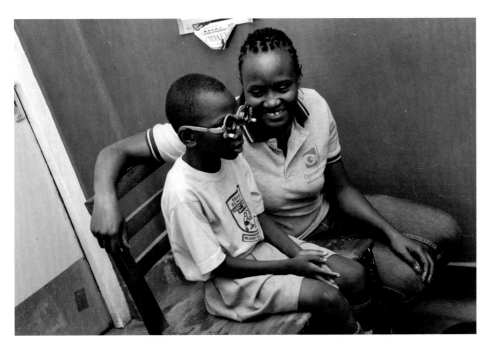

Emmanuel and his family thought he was blind until his eyes were examined by a teacher. Photograph courtesy of Brien Holden Vision Institute.

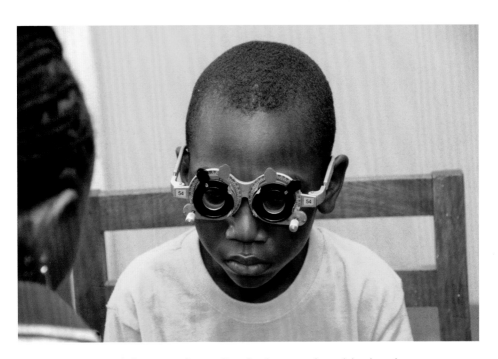

Emmanuel, from Uganda, was found to have a serious vision impairment that could be corrected with glasses. Here he is wearing trial lenses. Photography courtesy of Brien Holden Vision Institute.

A Kenyan patient having his lens imaged with a Peek Retina device.
© Rolex/Joan Bardeletti.

Anyone can do it. Here an untrained observer uses a Peek Retina device to photograph
the back of this patient's eye at an international conference. © Peek.

An image of the retina clearly visible after this patient's eye has been photographed with Peek Retina. © Rolex/Joan Bardeletti.

A Zipline drone takes off into the Rwandan skies, laden with emergency medical supplies.
Photograph courtesy of Zipline.

A Zipline drone drops off its life-saving consignment, a parachute ensuring a soft landing.
Photograph courtesy of Zipline.

A man uses the Folding Phoropter to test his eyesight in rural India. The lenses are placed in their designated position and the cardboard folded around them, forming a device resembling a telescope. The patient looks through it at a fixed distance from the target, moving the outer chamber inwards until the image comes into focus.

© L V Prasad Eye Institute.

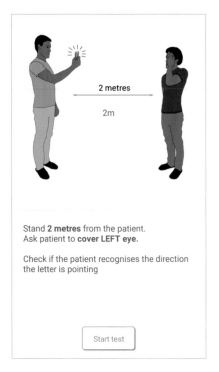

Stand **2 metres** from the patient.
Ask patient to **cover LEFT eye.**

Check if the patient recognises the direction
the letter is pointing

Start test

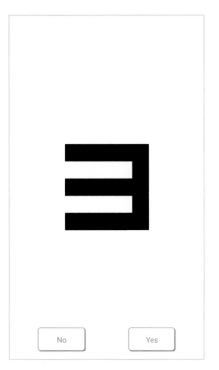

No   Yes

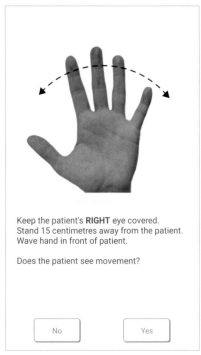

Keep the patient's **RIGHT** eye covered.
Stand 15 centimetres away from the patient.
Wave hand in front of patient.

Does the patient see movement?

No   Yes

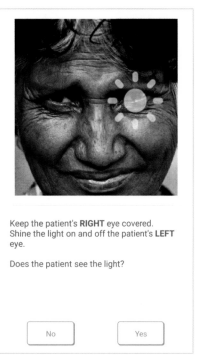

Keep the patient's **RIGHT** eye covered.
Shine the light on and off the patient's **LEFT**
eye.

Does the patient see the light?

No   Yes

Vula Mobile in action. A health worker guides a patient through simple tests for
visual acuity (including finger counting, hand movements and light perception),
and collects clinical data relevant for an ophthalmic specialist. The health workers
can use the app to share information with ophthalmologists who can give advice
on treatment or referral. Courtesy of Vula Mobile.

increased production and a reduction in poverty. But the lack of locally available eye-care services made that a difficult target and was costing the country dearly. Hundreds of thousands of its people suffer from uncorrected poor vision and most of this could be put right if only they had access to vision screenings and glasses.

In 2012, when VFAN launched our pioneering and ambitious programme in Rwanda, at least 90 per cent of its people had no access to local, affordable eye care. We were to find that well over a million of those only needed a simple pair of glasses to see clearly again. Many more could benefit from eye drops administered on the spot or a referral to a hospital for specialist treatment to prevent potentially blinding conditions.

With fewer than a dozen eye surgeons serving the whole country – primarily based in the nation's capital city – the scale of the problem faced by Rwanda was immense.

The big moment for Rwanda – and we hope this will be followed in the developing world – was when the government brought the Ministry of Health and the eye-care NGOs together to harmonise treatment.

This development can be traced back to 2009, when a group of Rwanda's eye-care NGOs signed up to a national plan for eliminating needless blindness.

Under the five-year plan, the Rwandan government aimed to provide eyeglasses at a rate of 400,000 per annum by 2012 and distribute 1.2 million eyeglasses by 2013.

By the time VFAN entered Rwanda for its first trial in late 2009, the government was already so far behind that Dr John Nkurikiye, the ophthalmologist in charge of delivering the plan, welcomed us with open arms despite our consignment of rather strange-looking adjustable glasses.

It's a testament to Dr John's pragmatism that he backed us when meeting with Dr Agnes Binagwaho, the Permanent Secretary of Health, even though the eye-care community had its grumbles at the time about adjustable glasses.

That was such an important meeting because upon trying on the glasses Dr Agnes declared that they were the best thing since sliced bread. She promised that we'd have her full support then and there and she has been our champion ever since.

It would not be an exaggeration to say that without the support of Dr Agnes over these years and her promotion to Minister of Health, VFAN would be in a much more difficult place.

Her role as a leader in the programme was critical and if our campaign is to succeed elsewhere we hope to find similar pragmatists in positions of authority. The solution – the cure if you like – for improving eye care is there – but only if countries are prepared to grab it. Dr Agnes has now moved on but we have every reason to hope for a similar close relationship with her successor.

So we put forward a plan to train nurses to provide adjustable glasses. This was revolutionary because the regulations required such treatment only to be given by the professional ophthalmologists and optometrists. Of those, there were few. At first, the Rwandan government did not endorse the programme and asked us to train nurses more comprehensively.

We asked Dr Ciku Mathenge, wife of Dr John and then an adviser to the World Health Organization, to develop a curriculum for Rwanda. After initial difficulties, a curriculum was agreed, including a section on adjustable glasses. This was the breakthrough we had been hoping for and the deregulation that will be needed across the developing world if we are to achieve our aims. The Rwandan government deserves great praise for its disruptive approach. Power to its elbow. John came to Murano with Ciku and quietly admitted to us over a sandwich lunch that he had not realised he needed glasses until he was preparing to train to become an eye surgeon.

VFAN ultimately developed an innovative programme to build and integrate locally available primary eye-care services into Rwanda's national health system by 2015. Being able to see clearly improves quality of life. Restoring people's vision has an immediate and tangible impact on their education, economic productivity, well-being and job security. Common sense dictates that anyone with corrected poor vision, like myself, would support such a programme. Yet funding and support for this initiative from the multilateral donor and aid sector proved impossible at first. Why was that?

Because poor vision is not a life-threatening condition, it comes invisibly low on the scale of public health priorities for development aid. Furthermore, development aid priorities are based on proven impact, and research on the impact of poor vision on productivity and educational outcomes was sparse then. Lack of funding interest means no research interest, resulting in no funding – a classic vicious circle. The World Bank supports literacy programmes teaching adults to read but it does not provide reading glasses. Strange.

However, once we were up and running and showing what we could do, institutional donors began to take an interest.

Over the past four years we have received financial support in the order of $330,000 from the UK's Department for International Development; $400,000 from USAID, the main American aid agency; a total of $1,400,000 from UBS Optimus, a foundation of the global private bank dedicated to helping children; and nearly $550,000 from other private donors.

But none of this could have started without family philanthropy. It could be called the philanthropreneur approach. I like to think VFAN combines moral commitment with the commercial imagination that we as business people have brought to it.

The programme's goals were ambitious: to make primary eye care (medication, reading glasses, innovative adjustable-lens glasses, and referrals for specialist treatment) permanently available to all Rwandans through the country's network of health centres – with the revenue generated from the sale of glasses (1,000 Rwandan francs or $1.50 each; free for the poorest 20 per cent) to be used by the ministry to sustain the programme beyond 2017, when VFAN's direct role would end.

And this is what we have achieved. VFAN has worked for four years with the Rwandan Ministry of Health to establish local primary eye care for the estimated 90 per cent of Rwandans – nearly 11 million people – living in nearly 15,000 rural villages who previously had no access to eye-care treatment.

In just five years, the ministry and VFAN have completed the development, implementation and integration of a nationwide primary eye-care programme, the first of its kind in the world. By March 2017, they had trained over 2,500 nurses nationwide working at all 502 centres, four in each. By the end of July 2017, they had provided over 2 million screenings, dispensed over 1 million eye drops for common problems such as conjunctivitis, dispensed 50,000 glasses

– primarily simple and inexpensive reading glasses – and referred more than 200,000 patients for specialist treatment, often vision-saving surgeries.

VFAN has succeeded because it thinks and operates in a way that would resonate with a commercial enterprise: it regards return on investment as critical; it sets clear goals; and it measures outcomes against targets at every stage. I hope my financial assistance has given it the flexibility to adapt strategy when needed (and the strategy did change quite radically over the course of the programme period). The arrival of Tom Rosewall to head VFAN in February 2014, bringing with him thirty years of business experience, commercial expertise and an outsider's perspective, proved a turning point.

I would argue that VFAN's firm, business-driven approach is different from many NGOs, who are often seen as slow and bureaucratic, and my funding allowed experimentation and changes of strategy and tactics in a way institutional funders today could not accommodate. We are the only eye-care NGO in Rwanda to operate nationally in all thirty districts and in each of the 502 centres.

We are motivated by a sense of urgency and a desire to render ourselves obsolete. As Tom Rosewall says: 'We're actually in a way the anti-NGO. Our aim is to create an integrated service for the government that makes our presence no longer required.'

Tom, an outspoken Californian, believes in cooperation with well-run governments. He also suggests there are 'too many NGOs spreading themselves too thinly across many nations with limited impact in any one; we chose to go deep in one, with unprecedented results'.

He insists on calling those helped by VFAN 'customers' rather than 'beneficiaries' and hits out at the practice of many NGOs which spend all of their annual aid in order to keep up levels for the next year rather than taking a more commercially driven approach focused upon return on investment for the nation and funders.

But Tom also asserts that there might be room for the 'Adam Smith approach' – in other words, free market economics – in the future if local entrepreneurs are galvanised to take on the sale of spectacles at the nation's 150 major markets. 'Why not? If companies make regular deliveries to the towns – clothes, food, Coca-Cola, whatever – one can envision how it could be worth their while to add glasses to their repertoire.'

VFAN invests in nurturing local Rwandan talent. It pays them well, funds continuing education for all staff for everything from language skills to advanced degrees, provides a work environment that encourages performance and accountability, and establishes confidence and a team culture of winning.

The innovative training course teaches general nurses, in just three days, to provide eye screenings, eye drops for infections and allergies, glasses, and referrals for complex cases.

The three-day course is revolutionary. Other countries, including those in Africa, prefer formal qualification routes that can take years. The Rwandan approach is an example of deregulation at its very best – reducing unnecessary costs and ensuring that millions more can access something that used to be exclusive.

The challenge was then to maximise awareness and uptake of the new service. We proposed a campaign of nationwide outreach to every one of the 15,000 local communities across Rwanda during a two-year period. This outreach programme is a mammoth exercise, working with and through a cross-section of civil society, including local leaders, hospital administrators and health centre nurses.

With well over 1 million people screened by the beginning of December 2016, this high-impact approach enabled VFAN to screen an additional 1 million people by the end of July 2017. While addressing the 'backlog of need' throughout the nation, it will maximise public awareness and generate a critical mass of repeat demand for eye-care services.

Previous efforts to deliver local eye care in other countries have failed to extend beyond local initiatives to a national level – in part because of poor service and a lack of medication and glasses. If a villager walks 10 kilometres for help only to find no glasses available, they are likely to tell their friends not to bother making the trip. VFAN has structured its local operation along commercial lines to optimise efficiency and ensure that medication and glasses are always available at each health centre.

It has built a marketing and sales team, working directly with 100 stakeholders in each of the thirty districts, and a supply chain reliably sourcing and delivering products to 502 health centres from their origins in Asia.

It orders the glasses through the international eyeglass distributors VisionSpring. They arrive at Kigali Airport and are kept in a warehouse close by. The $0.46 cost for each pair of glasses is paid by VFAN, which also pays for the nurse training and the outreach to villages. In future, when VFAN moves on, we hope that local entrepreneurs will take on the cost of the outreaches and distribute glasses across the country when they deliver other products. Clearly believes this approach can work across the developing world.

Most Rwandans pay 3,000 francs (£3) in health insurance annually, which contributes to keeping down the cost of the eye-care service, but the number of people who still decide against paying for glasses because of competing priorities or who are unable to afford them even after they have been prescribed is disappointingly high. Some 41 per cent of those who need glasses end up buying them, while 59 per cent of those who need them do not buy, although a proportion of them will still get glasses because they are considered poor enough not to have to pay. Breaking down the cultural barriers to wearing glasses remains a central part of Clearly's work, but ensuring that the glasses can be supplied to the places they are needed is a priority.

VFAN's aim in Rwanda has always been to play a catalytic role in quickly establishing eye-care services – the rapid deployment of resources combined with a well-defined exit strategy. Its work has been geared towards integrating the new eye-care services into Rwanda's national health system in line with the Rwandan government's goal of achieving 'operational independence' from NGOs and others in 2018.

To cement the status of the health centre-based service, VFAN has doubled the number of eye care-trained nurses at each health centre to four and is providing refresher training to all the nurses it has previously trained. The training course is now mandatory for students attending the nation's nursing schools and is so respected that it is part of the official degree curriculum for nurses at the University of Rwanda. VFAN has also mobilised the senior 'ophthalmic officers' based in each of the forty-one district hospitals to monitor and support the nurses at the health centres in their catchment areas.

Rwanda's Ministry of Health will assume full financial responsibility for new eye-care services from January 2018. For them, the business case for continuing the programme is strong. Detecting and treating eye conditions at an early stage – often preventing permanent visual disability – can save the ministry considerable amounts of money and relieve the burden on the limited number of hospital specialists (prior to VFAN's programme, half of patients visited hospitals solely to receive eye drops). Our pioneering model provides a template for other nations to rapidly address this global public health and productivity issue.

VFAN has worked with leading academics from the London School of Hygiene and Tropical Medicine and the Fondation Ophtalmologique Adolphe de Rothschild to critically assess the impact and effectiveness of the programme. We are studying how our work in referring patients for secondary and tertiary care has helped that sector, freeing up the time of the specialists to conduct the operations and other treatments that are needed.

The results will provide crucial evidence that will inform the scaling of the programme to other nations in Africa and Asia, with many nations on both continents interested in replicating VFAN's approach.

VFAN will not disappear from Rwanda. From January 2018, a core group will be retained to monitor primary eye-care services and provide technical support to the health ministry.

And there's further exciting news. VFAN is considering a plan to engage locally based entrepreneurs to act as distributors and salespeople of glasses, working alongside the trained nurses. This approach would leverage the clinical expertise of the nurses and the sales proficiency of the entrepreneurs to enhance the existing programme and sustain it for the future.

So let's go back to KG599 Street. For much of the rest of the week it is quiet here because Tuesdays, Wednesdays, Thursdays and Fridays are 'field days'. The team meets in the office on Tuesday morning. Depending upon the distance to travel, they may be going for just the day or staying overnight somewhere. The education and training team may be going to a specific district to conduct training – for new nurses, nurses that have moved to a new health centre, or refresher training.

The data dudes may be going to health centres to sort out irregularities in the reporting. The national coordination team could be doing a variety of things: meeting with district leadership to gain or maintain their support; visiting health centres that are underperforming; participating in district or local events where the overall primary care service and the outreach programme can be advanced. The teams usually arrive back in Kigali on Friday afternoons.

Then it all starts again on Monday, the critical day in the process. Time management is vital. If the data dudes point the teams in the wrong direction on Mondays and the teams ultimately end up going to places that don't require our attention, valuable time is wasted. We have till 31 December 2017 to complete this programme. Time is short.

We have to admit that conditions in Rwanda have been especially conducive to our work. We have had the enthusiastic adoption of the programme by the Ministry of Health, which is not afraid to try new approaches; the advantage that a majority of the country has health insurance, with comprehensive coverage provided by the state; and the fact that Rwanda has a low level of corruption is obviously a major help. And having a supply chain system already in place was the key. Conditions elsewhere will present different, perhaps larger, challenges.

None of that, I am glad to say, has lessened the appreciation of our achievements with this groundbreaking programme. We won top prize in the coveted International Aid and Development category at the 2016 UK Charity Awards. Of course I am pleased with that. But this is only the start. Now we must communicate the lessons of Rwanda and bring help to other nations in Africa, Asia and elsewhere. And we will.

EMMANUEL, SACKEY AND ASHA

Emmanuel could not attend school because he and his family thought he was blind.

Emmanuel, from Uganda, wished every day he could go with the other children in the village, but he had been nearly blind – or thought he had – since birth. He spent his days in his village, which he knew well enough to get around. His local community looked out for him to help him stay safe.

Emmanuel had a cousin, Yusuf, who used to tell him stories about school and other villages that Emmanuel could not visit.

Yusuf had good eyes and was very interested in school. He learnt one day that his teacher had been trained in screening the school children's eyesight. Yusuf had his eyes tested like all the other children, and all the while he thought of his cousin Emmanuel. He told his teacher about Emmanuel and sadly described his blindness.

Some weeks later, the teacher asked again about Emmanuel and gave him a note to take home to his aunt, Emmanuel's mother. A few days later, the teacher came home with Yusuf to meet Emmanuel. In the village, Yusuf found his cousin's mother so the teacher could talk to her.

Emmanuel had his eyes tested by the teacher and they discovered with great joy that he was not actually blind. He just had severe vision impairment which could be corrected by glasses. Both the little boy and his mother cried when Emmanuel realised for the first time he could see clearly wearing the trial lenses.

A few weeks later, still grateful for good news about her son and now also for his free spectacles, Emmanuel's mother happily made the arrangements for her son to go to school for the first time. This was something she thought she would never have the pleasure of doing. They were so grateful to young Yusuf.

Emmanuel is one of the many helped by the Brien Holden Vision Institute, named after its distinguished founder, one of the giants of the eye-care world, who died in 2015. Its chief executive is Professor Kovin Naidoo, another giant. Based in Australia, the institute is a social enterprise investing any revenues resulting from its work into trying to find scientific solutions and developing and delivering eye care and education programmes around the world.

Launched four years ago in 2012, the east Africa project, funded by Standard Chartered Bank under the Seeing is Believing programme, has been working to improve the quality of lives of children aged 0–15 years, and has been influential in the delivery of eye-care services, workforce development, policy change and creation of infrastructure.

Kovin spoke about the impact of child eye health:

Imagine a child who leaves home and, despite all the barriers of poverty, is able to get to school. On an empty stomach, maybe walking more than 2 km to get there, but when eventually arriving they are unable to see the chalkboard and find another barrier in this continuum of poverty.

Glasses rescued Sackey's studies

Sackey Vaness was having problems with his eyes and it had started seriously to affect his studies.

At junior high school in Denkyembour, Ghana, he started getting marks of 40 to 50 per cent when previously his lowest were 60 to 70 per cent.

Rather ashamed, he told his mother, who suggested he had stopped studying. He insisted that he had not and that the problem was he could no longer see to read and write as well as he had.

He attended a school health integrated programme run by Sightsavers and funded by the World Bank in four countries – Ghana, Senegal, Ethiopia and Cambodia. He was initially examined in school. The programme trains teachers to conduct eye examinations to identify children with problems. After he was examined, he went to hospital for refraction – to determine the prescription he needed.

Uncorrected refractive error is the leading cause of visual impairment, and accounts for 42 per cent of visual impairment globally, so it's an important part of the Sightsavers mission. It can have a serious impact on a child's education, given that 80 per cent of learning is visual.

That was the case with Sackey, who was provided with spectacles and is now a happy young man.

He says that he had been having problems for a year but had resisted his mother's appeals to go to the hospital. He felt a pain at the back of his eyes and tears came into them. Reading in the evening was impossible and he knew that his performance at school was deteriorating. Previously he had gone home, done his chores, slept and then woke up early in the morning to do more of his school work: 'But because of my eyes I couldn't learn. I felt myself getting behind in class,' he said.

He added: 'If I didn't get these glasses, my grades would have been very bad, I would have had a very bad future. When I put them on, I felt good, now I can read at night.'

He said he sometimes took his glasses off because people had told him if he wore them all the time his eyes would get small.

My grades have improved now, the exam I just did was good. I like maths and science. I was thinking about doing science but my mother wants me to be a pastor. I'd like to do biology, to be like people who work with the trees. I think I'll do agriculture science. I can see things more clearly with my glasses.

I feel very good about my glasses. Before I got them my mother was thinking about giving me some other medicine to make the pain stop but my grandpa told her I didn't need traditional medicine – I don't like the medicine, it's very bitter.

I'm in form 3, next year I'll go to the senior school. When I didn't have these glasses, when I started reading the exam papers I would feel the pain in my eye, and by the time I finished the exams it looked like everything was dark for a minute. If I got bad grades I don't think I could be myself, because when I got the worst mark and I showed my mother I felt ashamed.

Now Sackey thinks he will get 90 per cent next time round and does not mind getting teased by his friends, some of whom have also been given glasses. 'I think the glasses look nice but I feel ashamed because people look at me, even my friends. When I meet them they tease me about having a problem, but I just ignore them.'

Happiness is an operation for giggling Asha

Asha Mussa Abubakar, aged six, has problems that are more serious than Sackey's. She has come to stay with family friends in Zanzibar to get treatment.

Her story is told beautifully by Kelly Garrett and Sarah Filbey of Sightsavers.

Asha was born with cataracts in both eyes but the vision in her right eye is worse than her left.

Asha comes from Mozambique but has been living with family friends for four months and everyone is very fond of her. Asha's parents first thought that there was no cure for her blindness, and were very happy when they learned that there was a treatment available. Asha's grandmother brought her over but then went back to Mozambique.

Asha likes living in Zanzibar with the family and enjoys the company of the other children. Asha is very much looking forward to having her operation and being able to see. That is all she cares about right now. She would like to be able to read, and go to school.

Children in the village tease her but she doesn't let it bother her. One boy teased her for being blind and she told him: 'Well, I am going to have an operation and then I won't be blind, but you cannot have an operation to make your big head smaller!'

When Asha plays ball, it looks very much like she is looking away to the side, in another direction. She has absolutely no vision in her right eye, but the cataract in her left eye is smaller and centred, concealing the pupil. She has some peripheral vision in her left eye, so she turns her head to see directly ahead of her.

After a few minutes she was giggling and dancing and keen to show off her kicking skills. Suddenly we saw a glimpse of the girl and the personality hidden behind the hand across the eyes, and a propensity for childhood joy perhaps tempered by a sense of being different.

There's a nervous anticipation at the thought of Asha's response to surgery. We are all hoping for a transformation – not only in her eyesight, but in her confidence and level of happiness too.

On a Monday in late September 2016, Asha and other children are screened at Kibweni Hospital. She is dressed in smart clothes and is looking clean. She's usually covered in mud. It is good for Asha to see that lots of other children have the same problem as her.

The next day, the children go to Mnazi Mmoja Hospital. This is where the team will take over one of the operating theatres usually used by the ear, nose and throat department. The team will be doing four days of surgeries here. They have come over from Dar es Salaam, where they are usually based.

Today, there are eight children scheduled for surgery; Asha is fourth on the list. Asha is very calm. The children have not been allowed to eat since midnight last night. Some are restless and upset, but Asha is stoical and hasn't complained at all. In fact, Asha seems quite happy and we actually see her smile. When the nurse comes through to administer the eye drops, all the other children grumble or cry, but not Asha; she accepts them with a smile.

That is because she's actually looking forward to her surgery: she understands perfectly the potential positive impact a good result will have on her life. She has not noticed the hospital is right beside the sea. Would she like to see the sea after her surgery? Yes, she would. Finally, Asha can begin to anticipate enjoying herself, on the other side of surgery.

The first operation began just after 9 a.m. By 4.30 p.m., only the third surgery was under way. It's already been a long day and the children haven't eaten anything since midnight last night. They must be hungry, bored and miserable but it is only the small ones that grumble. Asha sits or naps quietly, she is calm and seems OK, but when she is finally taken into theatre she shows the first sign of fear. Asha becomes distressed and kicks and screams: 'I'm scared! I'm scared!' The nurses have to hold her down to administer the anaesthetic.

Dr Paul Nyaluke tells us that Asha's surgery has gone perfectly. She is in recovery coming round from the anaesthetic and then she will be taken back to the ward to sleep and eat.

We leave her to rest – it will be a big day tomorrow when the bandages come off.

The next day, Asha's eyes are covered with two big bandages. She slept well and has had breakfast but is still quite tired and sleepy. Her bandages are finally removed. Her eyes are sore and swollen but after the doctor checks them with his torch he tells us that everything looks good. She will have a full test in a few days once the eyes have recovered a bit more back at Kibweni.

Two days later, we return to see Asha, who is wearing a beautiful blue and gold dress. Her eyes look great. We notice that she is not covering her eyes with her hands, so this is a good sign, however small.

Asha goes in to see Dr Rajab for the final screening. The operation has been a success, he tells us; Asha can see. She can go home.

She is still quiet but seems to enjoy the drive. When we pull up at the house, she jumps out of the car, happy to be home.

When we say our goodbyes, for the first time since we arrived, Asha shields her eyes. We feel a moment of disappointment but we're told that it's become a bit of a habit that we hope she will break over time.

Asha calls out 'Bye!' and waves happily. Though she might have warmed to us a bit over the last couple of weeks, I think she's quite pleased to be saying a final 'Bye!'

What a wonderful story and I am grateful to Sightsavers for the fantastic work they do.

PASCAL AND REGINE

Sometimes Pascal Masengesho's patients treat him like a miracle worker.

And that is probably how he is regarded by Regine Mukasine, a Rwandan woman who recently started a job as a pre-school teacher after Pascal changed her life by prescribing her self-adjustable glasses which helped both her near- and distance-vision problems.

Pascal knows he is no miracle man, but it is hugely rewarding for him to play such an important part in the lives of so many of the people who come to see him.

Pascal is a nurse at Mukono health centre in the northern province of Rwanda.

I've told you several stories already about people who have been given fresh starts in life through the simple provision of eyeglasses or medicine for eye problems.

Now let's look at one of the people who have helped to make this happen.

Pascal, now twenty-eight, was one of forty nurses sent to Musanze, sometimes known as Ruhengeri, in northern Rwanda, back in 2012 for a three-day training course conducted by Vision for a Nation staff.

Ironically, it was Pascal, before he had received this training, who saw Regine and referred her to a hospital because he did not have the skills to do the vision testing himself.

He is one of 2,500 nurses trained by VFAN over the past two years.

Like Pascal, they will have been trained to examine the eyes, conduct vision tests, diagnose allergies and infections, dispense adjustable and reading glasses, refer complex cases and provide counselling.

So here is Regine's story. About 80 kilometres north of Kigali, the Mukasine family farm is carved into the side of one of Gicumbi district's ubiquitous hills. She is one of eight children. While at school in 2008, she began to experience bad headaches and watery eyes.

She did not know these were symptoms of a vision problem, since her sight had always been bad; instead, she thought that her regular tears were caused by the headaches.

She is bright and when Regine's parents saw her educational aptitude, they saved their money and sent her to a Catholic girls' secondary school, where she chose biology and chemistry as her specialist subjects and quickly became an outstanding student. Regine went down the science track because her dream was to train to become a nurse.

When the headaches started, she went to her local health centre at Mukono and was referred by none other than Pascal to the hospital in Byumba. It took her three hours to travel the 22 kilometres on foot, and she waited four hours to be seen. When she was finally examined, she described her symptoms to the hospital staff, and they simply prescribed her pills for her headaches and eye drops for the watery eye problem. The drops did not help at all, and the painkillers provided only temporary relief; the headaches and other problems continued.

For the next two years, Regine continued to buy pain medication from the nearest pharmacy. The problem became gradually worse until, in 2010, when she was preparing for her national examination, the headaches became so bad that she would get sick. The Catholic nun in charge of the students thought Regine was simply overworking herself as she studied for her exam, and ordered a day of rest. When Regine did not recover, the sister took her to the local health centre.

Regine was referred to the Byumba Hospital again, and once more made the 22-kilometre journey on foot. This time, however, she was seen by an ophthalmic technician, who used a torch to examine her eyes and conducted a vision test. He prescribed different eye drops and told her to return after one week if the problem did not ease. When Regine returned a week later, the technician conducted some further testing, then sent her to see an ophthalmologist in the same hospital.

The ophthalmologist conducted additional tests and prescribed a medication that was costly and difficult to find. Regine was able to buy the last dose of it available at the hospital, using her health insurance. The doctor told her this was the final thing he could prescribe before glasses, and instructed Regine to come back after two weeks.

The medication did not help at all, and Regine's headaches and eye problem became so bad that she could not see. However, she struggled on in her preparation for her school exam, and studied as much as she could tolerate: only about one to two hours per day.

When she returned to the hospital – only four days before her national secondary school exam – the doctor conducted a new test, this time having Regine read a chart with the aid of different kinds of lenses. He finally identified lenses with which she could see properly, and gave her the appropriate prescription. The glasses were only available in Kigali, but the doctor assured Regine that he could rush order them and get them to her within two days – just in time for her school exam – if she could come up with the money.

The cost of the glasses was the equivalent of $31. Regine called home to her parents to see if they could raise the cash, but they said they could not even borrow that much money in four days, given that almost everyone they knew was a subsistence farmer like themselves, and that kind of money was beyond their means.

So, Regine sat the national exam without glasses, with her eyesight and headaches at their absolute worst. She recalls bending all the way over with her nose just centimetres from the page to try to see the questions; even so, she could barely read the words, and developed a terrible headache from the strain; she could feel the blood pooling in her eyes, and the nerves pulling. It became nearly impossible for Regine to concentrate and to complete the exam. She did as much of the test as she could, but got to a point where she could not continue, and had to put her head down on the desk.

Students are allotted three hours to complete the exam, but despite trying her hardest, Regine was only able to complete less than half of the exam in about an hour. Incredibly, Regine passed it anyway but she did not score high enough marks to qualify for the scholarship she needed for nursing school.

After the national school exam, Regine returned home. She continued to experience all the same vision problems as before; her painful symptoms persisted, but since she was not reading and writing as much any more, they were less acute. She worked on the family subsistence farm.

One day, Regine's father returned home after being called to the local health centre for a meeting of the community health workers and announced he had good news. He told Regine that he had learned about a new programme that had recently trained nurses from their local health centre, and that these nurses could now screen people and provide glasses as needed, locally, for only $1.50 with health insurance. He told her to go to the health centre.

Regine was instantly filled with hope and excitement; she could not wait to get the glasses she knew she needed. She spent a week procuring the money and then went to the Mukono health centre as soon as she had it in hand.

She was seen and tested by Pascal, our miracle-working friend!

He conducted all the tests the ophthalmologist had performed at the hospital – including testing her vision using different kinds of lenses – and ultimately prescribed Regine a pair of adjustable-lens glasses that he dispensed on the spot. Since her problem was both seeing far away (like the chalkboard in school) and reading, Pascal helped Regine adjust the lenses until she could see both far and near.

As I have explained, Vision for a Nation has pioneered adjustable-lens technology that allows glasses to instantly focus at the turn of a dial. While the majority of Rwandans need only basic reading glasses, adjustable-lens glasses provide an immediate, life-changing solution for people with more complex vision problems, like Regine.

Once Pascal had helped Regine get the glasses adjusted properly, he made her practise reading and walking around. 'At that moment, I was so happy because I could read clearly and see better,' Regine recalls.

I was really happy, and I felt hope, because I knew that I was going to be able to see.

I was really happy, too, because once I went home and used the glasses more, the dizziness went away little by little, and my headaches also started to go away.

The glasses changed my life, because they helped me to see, to read, to write, and to stop the headaches.

There is a big difference now, because I can see, and the headaches have reduced... Because something has changed – I can see now, and before I could not! – my life is different: before, I used to get headaches all the time, so I could not work; now I can work without any problems. I feel like if I was able to go back to school, I would be able to study and perform better.

The Clearly team caught up with Regine again recently. She is now teaching at the local nursery school for 3–6-year-olds every morning. She has a son called Prince and he goes to work with her.

It is still her dream to become a nurse, and she is saving up to go to nursing school.

Pascal played a significant role in Regine's life, because he sent her for the original examination and then helped her to adjust to glasses after he had been trained to prescribe them some time later.

Regine's predicament is one faced by many people around the globe: if you cannot see, you cannot study or learn effectively. Visual impairment can be a barrier to realising the full extent of a student's educational aptitude, thus shackling the potential of individuals like Regine and perpetuating the cycle of poverty in many nations.

Pascal says the training was easy to understand because it was delivered in the local language of Kinyarwanda. 'I used to think after graduating from nursing school that all eye problems could be treated with antibiotics because that was all that was available in the health centre. Now there are new drugs available and we are able to prescribe and deliver glasses.'

After the training, Pascal and other nurses met with community health workers to spread the word that eye services were now available at the health centre. 'It was difficult to sit in front of patients and be unable to do anything for them because of a lack of skills. Now we are more confident because we feel so much more useful.'

They used to refer all patients like Regine to Byumba Hospital because they did not have the resources to address eye problems. Now, new patients are coming in every day seeking eye-care services. With vision services available and affordable locally, older people no longer have to spend hours travelling over difficult roads to be prescribed glasses they would have difficulty in affording anyway.

Pascal says that people think the health workers at Mukono have a new power to restore their sight because these services were not available before and they have suffered for a long time.

He can think of at least six patients he consulted recently who had remained at home for years, in some cases decades, because there was nothing the centre could do to help their vision problems.

'When patients have had poor vision for a long time and then I give them glasses, it is like I am witnessing miracle after miracle.' He recalls seeing his patients time and again jump up from their chairs, amazed that they can see, praising God and thanking him for the wondrous restoration of their sight.

How wonderful it would be if we can make Pascal's story the norm throughout Rwanda, and then move on to make it the norm in other countries as well.

PART IV

THE SECOND OPTICAL REVOLUTION

CHAPTER 11

ON THE EDGE OF CHANGE

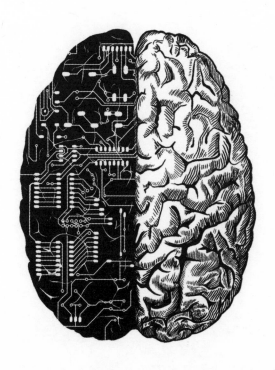

The age of the driverless car is upon us. So it should not surprise us too much that before long, machines will be able to diagnose serious eye conditions quicker and more accurately than physicians.

I find this one of the most exciting developments since I became involved in the world of eye care, one that will be of huge benefit to those who are responsible for care and, more important, those who need it.

It is all about artificial intelligence, or AI, the development of computer systems able to perform tasks which have always been seen as requiring human intelligence.

What is happening is that DeepMind, the artificial intelligence arm of Google, is collaborating with the world-famous Moorfields Eye Hospital close to the City of London to build a system that will detect early signs of degenerative eye conditions like diabetic retinopathy and age-related macular degeneration.

Moorfields has shared a million anonymous eye scans with DeepMind - based in King's Cross, just around the corner from the Clearly headquarters. Its researchers are painstakingly using the information to build an algorithm that will eventually enable doctors to cross-reference symptoms and signs of disease and pair that information with features of the images of the retina.

One day, I hope, doctors all over the world - including the developing world, on which Clearly is heavily focused - will be able to take advantage of this machine-assisted 'deep learning'. Organisations like Vula Mobile, winner of the Clearly Vision Prize, have shown us how the results of screenings taken by health workers or nurses can be shared instantly with specialists anywhere. So people identified at the primary eye-care level with which we are most concerned will also be the eventual beneficiaries.

To put it as simply as I can, an eye doctor will have a finite number of patients in his or her career and will rely on their experiences with those patients to advise new ones. But the information we get from thousands and thousands of scans and their relation to images of the retina will make that advice sounder and obviously more accurate. It is a revolution.

And it is needed pretty quickly, precisely because of recent big technological developments in ophthalmology.

In the past few years, the scanning of patients' eyes using OCT – optical coherence tomography – has grown rapidly. These three-dimensional scans of the retina are much better at detecting eye diseases than the imaging used in the past.

Now, the problem is that while an increasing number of opticians have these scanners, they don't have the experience or knowledge to interpret the scans. This means that as soon as anything unusual is thrown up by the scans, the opticians feel they have to refer the patients to hospitals to be seen by specialists. The danger then is that the system overflows and the people who really need the treatment have to wait while other, less urgent, cases are dealt with. Conditions like macular degeneration and diabetic retinopathy – if you are diabetic, you are twenty-five times more likely to go blind – have to be treated quickly, preferably within days. These two conditions affect many millions of people globally and without treatment many of these individuals will go on to become visually impaired or blind.

The kind of information thrown up by the DeepMind research will make it so much easier for the doctors to prioritise the cases that really do need urgent treatment. If you take a million scans which have been shown to many of the world's leading doctors, assemble them all in one place, and put them into a machine and build your algorithm, the system will have the benefit of thousands and thousands more experiences than any one surgeon or even a group of surgeons could ever have.

How long will it be before the system is in place to help the eye world? I hope not too long. I am told that DeepMind is close to producing a paper on its research project which will then be subjected to scrutiny by peer-reviewed journals. Then there will be the customary medical trials, and then let us hope that we can get this up and running as soon as possible.

DeepMind, aware of understandable public concern about the privacy of records, stresses that all the information it has been provided with by Moorfields is anonymised.

An executive emphasised to me that comprehensive steps have been taken to make sure the data is depersonalised. They are also historic scans and will be used to improve future care and not the care any patient is receiving today.

This kind of groundbreaking research cannot happen without data and although DeepMind is clearly sensitive to privacy concerns, it is obvious there is little risk of a breach here.

My hope is that when the neural system is ready, everyone will take advantage of it. In fact, if I was a patient I would certainly ask questions if my specialist was not using it. As one DeepMind executive said to me:

Most sight loss is preventable provided you can deal with it early enough. This advance should help us make those early interventions. As with uncorrected refractive errors, it is not as if there is no cure for these diseases. AI can help get those cures to the people who need them as speedily as possible.

Let me tell you about a conversation one of my colleagues, Graeme MacKenzie, had with a student at an event organised by One Young World, a global forum for youth leaders, in early 2017. She asked about the ethical issues surrounding the use of AI for diagnosing conditions, and particularly if medically unqualified people get to use this sort of AI to make decisions about whether someone should be referred or whether they should get a pair of glasses. His response was that one day these algorithms will be so robust, so well-trained and so adaptive that it will be unethical not to use them, regardless of whether they are being wielded by physicians or by teachers.

And There Are More...

So that is one idea for the future – but not, I hope, for the distant future. Other organisations are planning advances which, although starting in the developed world, will be extended elsewhere eventually. At a Wired Health conference in early 2017, for example, a new company called Give Vision showed how it is developing an electronic headset to help restore sight for the 165 million people with eye diseases. They are developing goggles and glasses that provide a hands-free solution designed for home or office use and offer the ability to enlarge text and enhance the remaining sight for people with limited vision.

They have a stated aim of helping people in the developing world as well as the developed countries, but it is unlikely to be available on the NHS before 2025.

Another start-up was Ophthorobotics, presented by Franziska Ullrich, which is a robotics solution to a straightforward procedure necessary in addressing macular degeneration. They are focused on the US, Japan and five countries in Europe, including the UK. It is interesting for Clearly because it is another new technology that could help free up the time of practitioners and produce higher patient safety.

As always, however, these new initiatives have to get past the eye 'establishment'. Opternative, the world's first 'online eye exam' service, was rolled out across twenty-seven states in the US in 2015 but has run into all kinds of trouble. The eye-care establishment in some states want to ban them.[29]

The service offers users a refractive eye exam of up to twenty-five minutes' duration, using a computer to view tests and a smartphone to record results. A prescription, validated by a state-registered ophthalmologist, is issued within twenty-four hours after payment of a fee.

Developers said that a clinical trial it had carried out found a 'strong correlation' between its own eye exam software and traditional in-practice refractive eye exams, delivering 'statistically equivalent patient satisfaction' and visual acuity with the resulting prescription.

But American optometrist leaders have warned over the potential dangers of splitting the refractive and in-person practitioner elements of eye testing. They argued that an online system could never be an adequate substitute for an appointment with a fully trained healthcare professional.

I differ with the experts here. They argue that the average consumer will stop going for eye health examinations if they can get their prescriptions online. Yes, there is a risk that there are people who don't realise that a prescription is only a small part of the larger eye exam, but in truth this risk can be mitigated by public campaigns that promote eye health. For example, rather than banning these new technologies, why not require that the companies that develop them must – by law – promote the importance of getting regular eye exams in all their advertising and marketing material? Why make the customer suffer for the fact that the eye-care community has struggled to convince the public of their value to their health?

And what about an optometry app that allows you to perform your own eye test? 6over6, hailing from Israel, is a vision care app that helps users to carry out their own eye tests. Its venture, Glasses On, won one of the nine innovation prizes at the Clearly Vision Awards in 2016.

It provides a simple and intuitive smartphone app for a complete and accurate measurement of the refractive error of the eye, for eyeglasses or contact lens prescriptions.

The company says one of its goals is to revolutionise eye-care access in the developing world. The app enables you to measure the refractive error of your eye through the manipulation of light. You can use the app to get a complete prescription for far-sighted or near-sighted vision, pupillary distance and astigmatism.

And in that excellent EYElliance report that I have highlighted elsewhere in this book, there are descriptions of a plethora of innovations already coming into operation.

The report agreed with Clearly that developing easy-to-use, affordable handheld technologies, including smartphone apps, could reduce the complexity and drive down the cost of providing eyeglasses. These new technologies perform two distinct functions: first, they enable people with very little training in eye care to rapidly conduct visual acuity tests to determine who needs further evaluation; and second, they offer a fast and accurate way to determine prescriptions via handheld auto-refractors, and at a fraction of the cost of table-top auto-refractors.

Use of either function could potentially increase cost-effectiveness and expedite the identification of individuals with vision problems, thereby enabling low-skilled technicians to connect them to the appropriate care.

The report highlighted Peek's mobile application, which, when paired with a lens adapter, turns a smartphone into a retinal camera that can be used to identify certain eye diseases in children: in 2015, some twenty-five teachers across fifty schools used the device to screen 20,000 children, all in less than two weeks.

QuickSee, developed by the Massachusetts Institute of Technology, is one example of a new handheld prescription determination device. It has been shown not only to compare well with larger commercially available auto-refractors, but also to produce results that agree with the prescriptions determined by a trained refractionist.

In a 700-patient study conducted at the Aravind Eye Hospital in India, 75 per cent of prescriptions determined by using the device agreed with those issued by a trained refractionist. QuickSee will be offered at a price appropriate for adopting it in settings with limited resources, where it can be used by either low-skilled technicians to conduct out- reach, or trained eye-care professionals to increase access to eye care at primary care vision centres or more remotely located optical stores.

Lenskart, an Indian optical company, currently uses an- other handheld auto-refractor. The company has launched a training programme that equips individuals who have had no previous eye health education with the necessary skills to use this device for determining prescriptions.

These are select examples of companies that have devel- oped technologies designed to respond to specific needs in less developed countries and emerging markets, or that have been tested in these regions. Now let's turn our attention to the practical steps that we collectively need to take to ensure that every country in the world has the capacity to deliver universal eye care.

FELICIEN

Five years ago, Felicien Senzoga's life hit a crisis.

Ten years earlier, he had moved from the Musanze district in the northern province of Rwanda in search of work so that he could put his children through school. At that point he had two; now he has five.

He had been trained in tailoring work and got a job at a textile factory in Kigali.

But then he ran into serious vision problems and, in his own words, feared that he would be fired because he was costing his colleagues and bosses money.

Good eyesight is essential for Felicien. For nine hours a day, six days a week, getting a salary equivalent to $57 a month, he is one of a group of tailors, sewing or embroidering one item on an article of clothing at a time – maybe a button or button hole, a sleeve, a collar – before passing it on to the next tailor in the chain, who sews the next item.

Felicien, aged forty-seven, and his colleagues have a daily group quota, and get paid according to the number of items they sew within the group. If they don't meet their quota, the whole group is paid half their normal daily wage; so, in a very real sense, Felicien and his co-workers are dependent upon each other's job performance.

Good vision is important for every aspect of his job but without it, threading a needle, which he does dozens of times per day, is nigh-on impossible. He has to hit the spot to avoid missing the hole and breaking the needle on the button.

Felicien's vision began to deteriorate in August 2011. He recalls noticing it for the first time while threading a needle; he felt strain on his eyes and a headache beginning as he struggled to do it, and ultimately needed to pull back in order to see the needle and thread clearly.

He lives with family on the outskirts of Kigali. As you approach their home, the first thing you see is 'Happy Sam' emblazoned on the outside walls of the house. Felicien and his wife named their youngest child 'Happy Sam', and Sam's siblings have inscribed his name on either side of the front door, so that you enter surrounded by Happy Sams – imparting an immediately warm impression of a happy home.

Felicien loves his family; he is the sole income-earner for the seven of them. In his spare time he enjoys reading – especially news sources and his Bible – and is also a reader at his local church.

Sunday is Felicien's favourite day of the week, because it is their family day. Felicien goes to church on Sunday morning with his family, and spends the afternoon helping his children do their homework – particularly his two eldest daughters.

So, on a Sunday in February 2017, the Clearly team paid a visit to Felicien and his family. Surrounded by young Samuel, Maurice, Soleil, Eminante (the French names a reminder of Rwanda's Belgian past) and Esther, he told his visitors that when his eyes began hurting he knew it was a serious problem.

Over the next two years, his concern grew proportionately to his worsening problem. 'I was worried because I was not performing properly at work,' he says. 'It would take twenty minutes to do what previously took me seven minutes.'

During this time, Felicien did not seek treatment because at first he did not think that his vision problem was that serious; then, once it became unbearable, he did not have the financial means to pay the cost for the exam and glasses, which he estimated amounted to several months of salary and almost a year of savings. 'When I get paid, I first think about my family and their needs,' he says, and with a family of seven and a modest salary, there is almost never enough money left over for unexpected costs.

'I was worried I would lose my job,' he recalls. There are no comparable alternatives for the kind of work Felicien does. He recognises that 'changing from one industry to another is difficult', and even if he had been able to find a new job quickly – which is always a challenge, particularly in a country with a high unemployment and even higher underemployment rate – 'it would not have been easy for me to find a new line of work and to start life [again] outside of this industry'.

'My family's life would have gone backwards, because I am the one who provides for them, so they are dependent upon my job. There is no other income or financial help that we get; it is only me.'

He feared his children would not eat properly, or dress properly, or be able to pay school fees or go to the hospital when sick. Given the high value he places on his children's education, Felicien especially worried that 'their life in school would change; if a kid doesn't eat, they can't study properly because their ability to think changes'.

One day at work, Felicien and his colleagues were told that a team of nurses was coming to screen all workers over forty, and wrote their names on a list, including his.

The following day, after registering each participant, the Vision for a Nation team started screening people one by one. Felicien recounts:

> When it was my turn, they asked me what my vision prob-lem was and I explained it to them. Then they did the test and gave me this paper [a prescription for glasses]. They told me that this number, +1.5, indicated the strength of glasses I needed, and that I could take it to a health centre anytime in the future and get glasses.

Felicien recollects the moment the technician conducting his exam gave him the correct glasses to try:

> I could suddenly see clearly, without struggling. Before, when doing the test without glasses, I could not read at all; with the glasses, I could read the chart without trying hard at all ... At that moment, I was happy; It made me happy and gave me hope that my life would continue.

Now, when using his glasses at work, Felicien says he can see the needle and thread perfectly clearly. This has had a positive impact on every aspect of his work: 'I don't have to strain my eyes now, and I can work without getting tired ... before, I would get tired from the strain, but now when I put on the glasses, the work goes easily.' Whereas it used to take him five minutes to thread or re-thread a needle, it now takes him only one minute, and what used to take him twenty minutes to sew now takes him only seven minutes. This is good not only for his own job performance, but also for his colleagues, his employer and his job security.

Felicien and his family smiled happily as he told the Clearly team that glasses had improved his productivity at the factory and meant that his workmates could earn more as well.

However, his smile vanished when he told us how seriously worried he had been that he would lose his job when his vision began to fail. 'I was scared. It looked like we would have to return to Musanze. Then the health team came and my life was changed.'

He adds that his fellow workers were asking when the team of nurses would go back to the factory, because others had seen how glasses had helped him and were hoping they could acquire them as well.

And his children have benefited so much. 'I have been able to help them with their homework again and I am so happy that they have improved their grades. I want them to develop and have a good life.'

Felicien's situation is one faced by many people around the globe: if you cannot see, you cannot work or learn effectively, perhaps at all. Visual impairment is a major barrier to securing and keeping paid employment, and thus shackles the potential of individuals like Felicien and perpetuates the cycle of poverty in many nations.

People living in low-income countries (where 90 per cent of the world's visually impaired live) and older workers (as near vision commonly deteriorates after the age of forty) are those most likely to face vision problems. Both risk factors were true of Felicien, who was one of the 2.5 billion suffering from uncorrected refractive error. However, the good news is that 80 per cent of all visual impairment can be avoided or cured, and refractive error – the most common cause – can be corrected by glasses in over 90 per cent of cases.

After hearing that this programme is also available at local health centres, Felicien said:

> I felt so happy that I went back home and told my neighbours about it; I showed them my glasses and told them about the organisation that gave them to me, and I told them how all the health centres in their area now have these services, [and] I encouraged them to go; I told them how the glasses had helped me resolve my problem, how without them, I cannot read at a normal distance, but now, with glasses, I can.

Since then, two of Felicien's neighbours have gone to the health centre and obtained glasses.

The fact that this programme has made glasses available at local health centres has been a relief to Felicien himself, he says, 'because I know that if I lose my glasses, I will be able to get new ones easily and affordably'. In fact, ever since the day that changed his life, he has carried the prescription in his wallet, so that he can replace his glasses immediately should that ever be necessary.

CHAPTER 12

THE
ANSWERS
IN SIGHT

T

HE

ANS

WERSI

NSIGHT

Putting right the scandal of billions of people never being given the chance to see clearly will require action on many fronts.

But it is not for the lack of a cure that this sorry state of affairs has been allowed to continue over centuries. For 700 years there has been an answer – glasses. The problem has been an inability on the part of world governments and health organisations either to understand that so many people are suffering, or to comprehend the benefits to individuals and their countries of helping people to see. At the same time, the private sector has utterly failed to take advantage of this market opportunity for glasses in the developing countries. There is a massive untapped need for low-cost glasses.

We have considered the four Ds – diagnosis, distribution, dollars and demand – and seen why each of them pose obstacles to the achievement of access to glasses for all. All of them place avoidable high costs in the way of a solution.

But while they are obstacles, they are not an excuse for inaction. I fear they have been used as such for too long. There can be no excuse for the fact that the world has continued to ignore this problem – the absence of a commitment to improve the world's vision in the UN development goals being the latest example – or for the eye-care establishment being unwilling or reluctant to make the changes that would bring relief to so many because they have not liked seeing their jobs done by less qualified people.

I believe the answers are within sight, and that with hard work, will and invention, a solution can be reached – and reached quickly.

In the course of writing this book, we have consulted experts in the eye-care world and many other fields, including retailers, supply chain analysts, communications and campaigning chiefs and even futurists.

I am making proposals which, though they may take time to be developed and worked through, would undoubtedly slash costs eventually and help us towards our goal of access to glasses for all. Some, including those in the next chapter, should be achieved quickly. Others are more medium-term, and some are longer-term, but all are more than feasible before a human lands on Mars.

It is a vision, yes, but one that I believe can be achieved. I would be the last to claim I have all the answers.

The poor and underprivileged have not always benefited from industrial and technological advances. Seven hundred years ago, glasses were cutting edge; today, a third of our population still doesn't have them. The second optical revolution is aimed at relieving the plight of those people. As the world continues its unstoppable search for disruptive breakthroughs, they cannot be allowed to miss out again.

So here, in the next four chapters, is my blueprint, based on my fourteen-year journey untangling the knots in the convoluted yarn ball of the current eye-care world, eighteen months of the Clearly campaign and hundreds of hours of conversation with people involved in the quest for answers.

As I said, there is no silver bullet. But there are enough bullets here to help shoot down our enemies – inaction, ignorance and self-interest.

CHAPTER 13

DIAGNOSIS: IN THE PALM OF YOUR HAND

It will have become crystal clear to readers by now that there are not enough eye specialists in the developing world to do the jobs that we in the developed world take for granted.

Until this basic fact is understood by governments and accepted by the profession, we cannot get far.

In some African countries, there are just a small handful of eye-care professionals. When I last checked, there was not one ophthalmologist in Sierra Leone. And even where there are optometrists and surgeons, they will live in the big cities and not in the rural areas where there are so many problems and where many have never had an eye test in their lives. But task-shifting will allow the limited number of busy specialists we have to do their jobs at hospitals, clinics and health centres.

In countries like Rwanda and Bangladesh, nurses and health workers are already screening people for vision errors and handing out glasses for those with straightforward problems. In Rwanda, they have distributed hundreds of thousands of reading glasses and self-adjustables for distance problems. A three-day training course gives those nurses the required skills to screen people for problems, and they do it very efficiently, as we saw on our field trip to Rwanda, which I described earlier.

I believe governments across the world must follow the example of Rwanda, Bangladesh and other countries and allow non-specialists, including specially trained nurses and health workers, to test the eyesight of their people. The 'establishment' should drop its objections to such task-shifting and stop behaving – in the words of Brian Doolan – like a 'medieval cabal'.

I believe the use of smartphones to screen vision, and to detect refractive error and more serious eye problems, must spread across the developing world and not be confined to certain countries and age groups. Some 93 per cent of Africans have access to a phone, but few have access to eye care. The answer is staring us in the face. Peek Vision has set an example by allowing teachers in Kenya to test the sight of their pupils with smartphones. This must spread to a wider range of non-specialists. Give the nurses mobile phones.

And we must encourage more Vula Mobiles – the brilliant winners of our vision prize – to spring up all over the developing world. We would love more professionals – ophthalmologists and optometrists – to move from the developed to the developing world, but are realistic enough to know that this is unlikely. So companies developing apps like Vula – connecting health workers who have tested the sight of people in South Africa with experts in the big cities and outside the country – must be encouraged to flourish. If we can combine the Peek and Vula technologies, what a breakthrough that would be. What if we could develop low-cost, mobile tools and innovative computer vision techniques to enable non-experts in remote areas with little knowledge or training to conduct vision screenings and share the results with healthcare providers and other stakeholders?

In Bangladesh, BRAC (Building Resources Across Communities), one of the largest non-government development organisations in the world, has over the past four decades recruited nearly 100,000 frontline community health workers – the wonderfully named Shasthya Shebikas – to distribute basic health products like sanitary napkins, soap and condoms.

After the brilliant intervention of VisionSpring, they have added reading glasses to their sales basket and have distributed hundreds of thousands of pairs of glasses. And they have been trained to screen.

In Pakistan, female health workers travel to people's houses to carry out screening tests, usually on women who spend most of their time in the home.

In India, SeeChange, the social responsibility arm of the lens-maker Essilor, has organised an Eye Mitra programme which recruits, trains and supports unemployed and under-employed young people to become eye-care providers. Eye Mitra is Sanskrit for 'friend of the eyes' and it does a one-year optician training programme, two months of classroom study and ten months on the job. They learn about refraction, edging and mounting glasses, how to refer patients for specialist treatment, and business skills.

The huge advantage of Rwanda for VFAN and Bangladesh for VisionSpring was that they were building on already established distribution routes.

Michael Conway, a senior partner at McKinsey & Company, and head of its global public health practice, told us that, in some countries, public or non-profit supply chains deliver health commodities, such as family planning goods, to cities and towns, then private businesses distribute them to clinics, pharmacies and other retailers.

In some developing countries, community health workers are trained to deliver immunisation, medicines and family planning products, a model that could have potential for glasses. 'Often community health workers deliver seven or eight services and it is feasible that, with additional training, they could add eyewear to their services,' he said. Mobile technology to evaluate eyesight could also help supplement training. If the eyeglass supply chain followed other examples of lean operations, he agreed there may be potential for lowering costs by reducing the number of operators who charge for various steps in the chain.

And yes, as mentioned in Chapter 8, given that there are a number of countries that allow non-physicians to carry out cataract surgery, surely it is time to consider allowing the non-specialists to prescribe as well as dispense glasses, reading as well as distance.

Non-specialists are allowed to prescribe in Japan, and it works. Japan happens to be the country with the highest percentage of glasses wearers and it also boasts one of the world's best eye-care services. In Japan, the non-specialists leave the specialists to tackle eye disease and carry out operations.

So come on – if some countries allow trained nurses to operate, surely they must be allowed to prescribe everywhere. Countries that impose these restrictions should follow the more enlightened ones and lift them.

On the day that I wrote this chapter came the news I had been waiting for – news that I believe shows that the ideas I have raised in this chapter and later are feasible.

I have long admired Warby Parker, a New York company that sells fashion eyewear at lower prices by bypassing the traditional distribution model. It sells prescription eyewear direct to consumers via the internet. *GQ* referred to Warby Parker as the 'Netflix of eyewear' – with good reason. Their expertise in e-commerce helped them expand rapidly and within five years of its founding, Warby Parker was valued at $1.2 billion.

So I was thoroughly delighted when the company announced in May 2017 another transformational move that will shake up the market.

It is launching a mobile refraction service that allows its current customers to measure their visual acuity using an app. In the company's own words, it 'helps eligible folks with expired eyeglasses prescriptions get a new one – without setting foot in a doctor's office'. I'm a passionate advocate of deregulation, so you can imagine the pleasure those words gave me.

Consumers will be able to download an app from the app store and take a twenty-minute test on their phone or computer. They then send their results and current prescription to a Warby Parker-affiliated eye doctor who determines if their vision has changed since their last eye exam. If not, they will get an updated prescription within twenty-four hours that can be used anywhere. This is a brilliantly disruptive move by a company that has never been afraid to disrupt in the past. Power to its elbow.

Let us hope that this great step forward can be built upon. Anything that expands the availability of vision care to a wider population must be looked at positively. But these ideas have met with resistance in the past. As I explained in Chapter 11, Opternative ran into trouble with the optometrists, with the eye-care establishment attempting to ban their online vision tests. But the firepower of Warby Parker may be hard to repel.

I have called for local entrepreneurs to be able to collect, transport and sell reading glasses. As the internet becomes more and more used in the developing countries, those salespeople should be able to acquire them from an online sales platform similar to Amazon's.

Amazon is a groundbreaker. We should use its venture with the e-commerce specialist StoreKing in India to let consumers order glasses online on the 10,000 tablets supplied by the business to India's retail outlets and convenience stores. The tablets offer product information in the regional language. This is opening up a new customer base for Amazon. Let's get glasses onto the sales list. And we should persuade the entrepreneurs recruited by Amazon in areas where internet penetration is low to get their consumers to order glasses from Amazon.

One other thought here. Companies manufacturing and delivering in the developing world have a responsibility. They should make eye tests compulsory for their drivers, and pay for the glasses if they are required. The eye test could be a prerequisite to getting insurance. This will increase their productivity and mean that road safety is enhanced.

As I have acknowledged, allowing prescription glasses to be classified as over the counter (OTC) goods would be controversial. But if we are to go on and get glasses to all the 2.5 billion, it will be necessary one day.

At present, only reading glasses are classified as OTC devices. All other glasses are classified as prescription medical devices and must therefore be dispensed by trained professionals.

As long ago as 1982, the Office of Fair Trading (OFT) in the UK concluded there was no merit in limiting the OTC sale of glasses to reading glasses. The advent of technologies like Glasses On from 6over6 that allow people to measure refractive error at the touch of a button can only strengthen that case.

The OFT was given the task of investigating the entire optometry field after complaints from consumers that they were acting as a trade. Its recommendation that prescription glasses should be sold like OTC products was made after consultation with leading eye doctors, who concluded that selling prescription eyewear without the need for a prescription from an optometrist was just as safe as selling reading glasses without a prescription.

Under present circumstances, there are doubts over whether glasses would fit well into the supply chains of other big companies delivering in the developing world. Most are focused purely on logistics, getting items from A to B, whereas glasses delivery usually needs people to go with them to screen, prescribe and dispense, as David Chute explained.

However, once a bulk market was established, that could change. Rupert Ellwood of Waitrose suggested partnering with fast-moving consumer goods suppliers and drug companies. Such suppliers in India have created chains where they can deliver their brands to millions of kirana (convenience) stores. They are able to give the stores credit and are capable of delivery every day.

One supply chain expert remarked that although it pained him to say it, the distribution and sale of cigarettes was highly efficient. 'We cannot use them, of course, but all over the developing world there are entrepreneurs who make sure shops and stores never run out of cigarettes. Sadly, they are considered high-value items and they have a short shelf-life, but stocking and restocking regularly happens.'

So we have seen the advantages of task-shifting. Now let's give the non-specialists the tools to do the job efficiently and quickly.

Enter the smartphone as a key player in the vision battle. As we saw in Chapter 9, Peek Acuity is an app used to test eyesight easily and affordably with a smartphone as accurately as any traditional tests. It can be done by just about anyone, certainly any health worker, with knowledge of how to use a mobile. Let's use them everywhere. Peek's systems connect the data from the tests to service providers, patients and key people who influence the uptake of treatment.

Having detected poor vision, let's find out what's causing it. To do that, you need access to the back of the eye. Peek's Dr Andrew Bastawrous and his team have given us the answer. They have prototyped a 3D-printed, low-cost piece of hardware called Peek Retina which is clipped onto a smartphone and makes it possible to get high-quality images of the back of the eye. Let's get it out there, everywhere, and let's get teachers, nurses and health workers using it.

Let's use the great advances that our Clearly Vision Prize helped to bring to greater prominence. Yes, we want more Vula Mobiles – a revolutionary app that connects primary healthcare workers in remote areas with on-call specialists around the country and, eventually I hope, in other countries as well.

The app allows trained health staff to take and share initial screening results and scans with on-call specialists, who are then able to offer diagnostic treatment advice for eye problems, and now other conditions, across borders and from many miles away. The specialists don't have to travel to the villages; they arrive over the internet.

And, yes, let's have more Folding Phoropters. The paper phoropter, folded in the Japanese origami style, assesses various lenses during the regular eye test. The folding version was created specifically to help diagnose refractive errors quickly and cheaply in the poorer areas of the world. Lenses are placed in their designated positions in what is folded to look like a telescope, with an inner and outer part.

The patient needs to look through the device a fixed distance away from the designated target and then move the outer chamber inwards until the image just comes into focus.

We should all of us be encouraging companies in this field to innovate. NGOs, philanthropists and governments should allow them to compete for seed capital that will give us advances such as Vula, the phoropter and HelpMeSee, a pioneering venture which is planning to train eye surgeons using simulators.

And looking further, but not too far, ahead, artificial intelligence should eventually be used to detect eye problems. Companies like DeepMind, the AI arm of Google, which is building an algorithm that will eventually enable doctors to cross-reference symptoms and signs of eye disease and pair that information with images of the retina, are the future and should be encouraged.

That's task-shifting of a very radical kind. But radical change is what we need if we are to succeed.

CHAPTER 14

DISTRIBUTION: AS EASILY AVAILABLE AS A CAN OF COLA

It seems crazy that in the second decade of the twenty-first century, people in many parts of the developing world cannot go along to a shop in their local town or village and buy a simple pair of affordable glasses along with their bread, biscuits and Coca-Cola.

If they live in settlements many miles away from the shops, surely they should be able to buy them from the mobile convenience store when it makes its occasional visits.

The problem, as we saw in Chapter 3, is an industry with a complicated supply chain where mark-ups proliferate because too many people take a cut, making the final price for glasses – particularly those provided on prescription – utterly out of line with the average $3 cost of making them in China and elsewhere.

In many countries, this is partly due to regulations which are no longer relevant. I personally believe that restrictions on the sale on the open market of both prescription glasses and reading glasses should be eliminated. That is my ideal world solution. This would empower non-specialists to dispense glasses for short-sightedness, far-sightedness and astigmatism. There is really no difference between them, and there are nowhere near enough specialists in the developing world to handle the prescription and sale of these glasses.

If we trap ourselves in that paradigm, we will never correct this injustice. Glasses are an old-world solution in a new age of opportunity.

Scrapping regulations would crash the cost and break open the market. What will really make a difference is when a shop-owner in Ghana, say, can stock and sell prescription glasses for their customer in the same way they can currently sell reading glasses. Once this happens, the price of distance glasses, sometimes hundreds of dollars in the developed world, will come down to the same price as reading glasses: several dollars. There is no fundamental difference in the quality of structure of prescription glasses and reading glasses. But the sale of prescription glasses is protected historically on the grounds that an examination by a specialist could throw up evidence of eye disease that a layman prescriber and salesperson would not detect. But of course the same could be said of prescribing and selling reading glasses, which is largely deregulated. And it is that protection that is preventing the development of a free market, and therefore putting up prices.

An embarrassing consequence of this policy is that it is not helping at all the 200 million children in the developing world who need vision correction via the provision of negative-power lenses at a time in their lives when glasses can make the greatest difference to their education and life prospects. I am well aware that this is controversial with some of my good friends in the industry. So I realise this may be some way down the line, but in my Utopia all glasses should be classified as OTC medical devices.

But let's make a start with reading glasses – aim for the low-hanging fruit, if you like. In many countries, like Bangladesh and India, VisionSpring, the social responsibility body founded by Jordan Kassalow, concentrates on getting reading glasses to the millions who need them. That example should be followed across the developing world. Remember, organisations like VisionSpring, VFAN, Light for the World, Vision Aid Overseas and many others subsidise the glasses they deliver and sell as they strive to build a volume market for glasses that will naturally bring down prices. As I have described in Chapter 3, prices are much higher in areas where there are no subsidies. The relaxations I have suggested will further help the building of this market.

First of all, the lengthy and expensive supply chain that governs the distribution and acquisition of glasses in the developing world should be drastically simplified. Far too many stages in the process, with mark-ups at every stage, mean that the cost being asked of people is much too high – and we are talking about providing spectacles for some of the poorest people in the world.

As I explained in Chapter 3, glasses go through all manner of stages before they get on the nose of the user. There are some eight processes for reading glasses and even more for prescription glasses. Inevitably, the cost must rise with each extra stage.

We could help to drastically streamline the supply chain by giving local entrepreneurs the ability to take delivery of the glasses at the port of entry, screen potential patients, assess vision and then sell the reading glasses.

A shop-owner, say, would arrange to collect consignments of glasses from the port of entry. He or she would have reading glasses in stock.

The product could then be shipped directly from the manufacturing facility to the shop itself – they ought to be supplied in the same way the shop-owner's other products arrive – and the end user can pick them up at the shop when they next come by for their groceries. The entrepreneurs would also organise and pay for screenings of potential patients at camps in the rural areas, making sure that the glasses were available there for distribution.

VisionSpring's partnership with BRAC in Bangladesh should become a model for organisations in this field. They should look to partner with organisations like the amazing Shasthya Shebikas, who earlier this year hit the 1 million mark for pairs of reading glasses sold in Bangladesh.

They should 'piggyback' on organisations that already have networks of people selling baskets of health products.

And they should also look to follow VisionSpring's attempts to sell directly to emerging retail chains, for example pharmacies in Kenya. As David Chute, board member of VisionSpring, said: 'Show me a network of rural salespeople selling personal care products to people earning between $1 and $4 a day, and I will show you a great distribution partner.'

Helping to break open the market would mean that innovative delivery companies like Essmart, from Bangalore in India, would come to the fore.

Essmart, third-place winner in our vision prize, distributes life-improving products in the most convenient way possible. Too often, technologies that have the power to radically improve lives do not get to the people who need them. Essmart aims to fix this problem by getting essential goods like affordable reading glasses into local stores – shortcutting the system by going straight to the places where people already shop.

Essmart sells a wide range of vital goods, like solar lighting and smoke-reducing cook stoves, to rural communities. It does this by getting those products to 15 million local retail shops, which it says count for 90 per cent of India's $550 billion annual retail spend.

It has partnered with lens-makers Essilor, which is supplying it with low-cost reading glasses and UV-protective sunglasses, and has shifted 4,000 units of its products to date. As part of the collaboration, Essilor has trained Essmart's field staff.

Then there is Maza Transport, a venture that has developed a transport network of affordable leased vehicles, providing urgent transport to remote rural communities. It provides flexible, on-demand transport services in Ghana using motorised tricycles.

Medical emergency? Maza is on hand. And when drivers have downtime, they can turn their attention to other vital services, such as transporting glasses and optometrists to nearby villages.

The drivers must be on call as a kind of ambulance service twice a week. The drivers are free to use the tricycles as taxis the other five days out of the week, and after two years of paying a weekly fee to Maza, they will own the tricycles.

Those in need of emergency care can subscribe to Maza, which specifically targets families with pregnant women and infants, but anyone can use the service via a free phone number. Maza had been considering offering 'last-mile' delivery services for healthcare or consumer goods, but says it jumped at the opportunity to test the service with vision screening.

By establishing volume markets, first locally, concentrating on places like schools and centres of population where there is a ready demand, then regionally and then nationally, we can contribute to an international movement that will one day see people demanding their right to see clearly, and being granted it.

In future, distributors could even partner with the fast-moving consumer goods companies to get glasses into the regular supply chains across the developing world. Analysts say that once the open market is established, glasses are much more likely to rapidly feature in their inventories.

And if they are not being held up in customs, it will be so much easier to put them onto the lorries of the big commodity chains operating with tight supply chain timetables throughout the developing world.

That's the here and now, and it must be achievable here and now.

Looking further ahead, the delivery and supply chain system should be revolutionised as soon as possible, with distributors of glasses taking advantage of the network of drone ports that will spring up across Africa and elsewhere in the developing world over the next few years. Rwanda is already leading the way by using drones to deliver emergency medical supplies.

Rwanda is the first government to have signed a contract with Zipline, a California-based robotics company that has designed a fixed-wing drone to drop essential medical supplies to rural areas. It is already in operation, delivering emergency blood packages to far-off areas using a parachute that drifts into the dropping area without the drone having to land.

Will Hetzler, co-founder and chief operating officer of Zipline, said it operates seven days a week, 365 days a year in Rwanda, providing resupply and emergency deliveries of blood products to district hospitals and health centres, and was in active discussion with several other countries about launching the service. He said: 'The response from doctors has been extremely positive. Zipline's service allows them to reliably provide a better standard of care for their patients. Doctors especially appreciate that Zipline's rapid response time can be life-saving in a medical emergency.'

He added:

Drones could be an effective way to deliver eyeglasses to rural communities. Given their high value, specialised nature and light weight, eyeglasses have many of the attributes of a product well suited to drone delivery. For products like eyeglasses, drones offer several advantages over traditional ground transportation, including faster delivery, more flexible and scalable distribution, and potentially even lower transport cost.

Other dramatic developments are afoot that could affect the way all medical supplies are eventually delivered across the developing world. We've been talking to Jonathan Ledgard, former Africa correspondent of *The Economist*, who has founded a venture called Redline, which will use drones to carry cargoes of medical supplies between drone ports close to roads and dotted around the country.

There will eventually be a network of them, not just in Rwanda but, one hopes, across the whole of the African continent. Many believe the development of drone ports will be more cost-effective and speedier for Africa than one day managing to build roads to the remoter parts.

Now, of course, these drones have to be used first and foremost to save lives and get blood to where it is needed. But it takes little imagination to see how their services could soon be expanded and used to drop other supplies such as – yes, you've got it – glasses.

Jonathan told me that drones would add to the transport system and would not replace the bicycle, motorbike or truck. 'Cargo drones are just going to add an extra layer of connectivity, especially in poorer countries where there are not enough resources to build tunnels or bridges.'

217

He predicted that in tropical parts of the planet, most towns should have a drone port before 2030. Durability of design was important. A cargo drone would have to be a 'combination of a VW Beetle and a *Star Wars* fighter'. The end result was something futuristic, but very modular, tough and utilitarian. The history of aviation showed that you started with a military solution and ended up with a mass civil application.

Kovin Naidoo, head of the Brien Holden Vision Institute, is hugely enthusiastic about the opportunity drones bring to the eye-care world.

He stresses how drones could help massively in cases where people are tested at a hospital and found to need prescription glasses.

> Often they will have walked 10 miles to the hospital. That is 10 miles there and back. But if the prescription glasses are not there, they would have to come back again. But what about if there were several people waiting and the hospital ordered all the glasses at the right strength and told the customers that a drone would be dropping them two hours later? I think we would have satisfied customers.

Says Kovin: 'We must use all the technology that is available. This is a big task and everything must be incorporated into the system if it works.'

And how could we make sure the drones go to the right place? There is now an organisation that has worked out how to break the world up into 3 metre by 3 metre squares and to give each an address, and we spoke to them.

Called what3words, the organisation gives everyone in the world a simple and usable three-word address far more precise than any postcode could manage. Addressing around the world is poor and billions of people are without a reliable way to define where they live. For example, table.chair. spoon points to a specific three-metre square somewhere in the world. The system operates in English and thirteen other languages.

Co-founder Chris Sheldrick became frustrated with poor addressing when working for a company organising live music events. Bands and equipment kept getting lost. Four years ago, over a cup of tea with a mathematician friend, he tried to find an easy way of naming everywhere in the world. They worked out that a list of 40,000 words was enough to give every 3 metre by 3 metre square on the planet a unique three-word address. The words are sorted by an algorithm that takes into account word length, frequency and ease of spelling and pronunciation.

Chris enlisted the help of his friend Jack Waley-Cohen to devise the core algorithm, build the first wordlist and create a simple-to-use app and website.

Chris told me how this would work to help the 2.5 billion. Let's say one of our trained nurses or health workers screened people in a village in Ghana.

They would go equipped with the what3words app on their phone and capture the three-word address of each person told they needed reading or prescription glasses. Names and prescriptions would also be taken. When it came to delivery, the package would be addressed with the country, region and village and the three-word address. The delivery partner would quickly be educated on the system. Simple.

And so the drone would know precisely where to go. Eye care in the years ahead? Let's hope so.

That's the future, and not too far away at that. But for now, let's grab what we have in front of us. Let's mobilise governments to understand what they can do now. Let's get those glasses to the 2.5 billion.

Let's make a difference – now.

CHAPTER 15

DOLLARS: COST DOWN, LOCAL PRODUCTION UP

If we are to achieve our aim of helping the world to see before humans land on Mars, we have to use everything at our disposal, to seize on every innovation and explore whether it will help us.

In Chapter 14, I showed how existing infrastructure – people, vans, lorries and glasses-makers – could make a serious dent in this problem.

In this chapter we'll look at the problem of locally imposed duties and taxes, which in some cases double the cost of glasses, making them unaffordable for the consumer and slashing any real profit margin for the entrepreneur or shop owner. I'll also examine how encouraging more local production can reduce costs. And, looking further forward, and taking advantage of the digital age, the apparent emerging market in the 3D printing of glasses must be one such development that we must seize. More of that later.

We say, sweep away those duties and drastically simplify the supply chain. In those few countries where restrictions on the sale of reading glasses still apply, sweep them away as well. Immediately, without any other change, we could – and I say 'could' – take a 35 per cent slice out of this problem.

Twenty per cent of the 2.5 billion people who need glasses need nothing more than simple reading glasses. That's half a billion people. A further 350 million people need reading and distance glasses. So they would benefit from reading glasses. Reading glasses would not solve their vision problems altogether, but they could make a difference between them being productive at work or not.

And all of this could be done without any resort to the internet. The tools of the analogue age – the ship or aircraft that bring the glasses in, the vans and lorries that transport them to the shops, and the people who sell them – are enough to make this step-change. The remaining 1.65 billion need distance glasses.

If governments removed taxes and import duties on all forms of non-branded glasses, the cost in the countries that need them most would be slashed. In some countries, import duty is as high as 90 per cent. Remember that billions in Africa live on less than $2 a day, so the price must be small for them to be able to buy.

Governments should understand that making it easier for their populations to buy glasses would have massive economic and health benefits. Glasses should not be treated as cosmetic commodities attracting duties. The duties often also mean that the consignments of spectacles are held up in customs, sometimes for days.

It is great news, as Liz Smith, co-founder of EYElliance, told us, that the World Health Organization's department of essential medicines and health products is collaborating with her organisation on policy-level work towards eliminating duties on non-branded glasses. Commonwealth leaders, who meet in London at a summit in April 2018, and more than half of whom wear glasses, must grasp this nettle.

Customs duties on glasses in America are around 2.5 per cent but in countries desperately in need like Kenya and India they are frequently taxed at around 10 per cent. Glasses in many developing countries are classified as more expensive 'health and beauty' products, without appropriate classification for non-branded eyewear.

But as well as reducing the cost of glasses, think of how we could be helped if glasses could be manufactured locally and cheaply in the countries that most need them.

This is not a dream; it could be a reality.

I have mentioned how prescription glasses – those prescribed by a doctor – are more expensive than reading glasses; usually too expensive for the people who need them.

An important initiative is under way to reduce the cost. There are a number of companies like Contour in China that have invested in methods of lens manufacture that ensure that prescription lenses are ready for use right away, without the need for additional processing steps (like the cutting of grooves around the edge of the lenses to ensure that they are held in place in the frame).

By avoiding the need for the sort of secondary processing that would traditionally be carried out by lens laboratories, these manufacturers are offering the potential to simplify the supply chain for prescription glasses and provide – one hopes – a means of bringing the cost of prescription glasses more in line with reading glasses. The larger the production volume, the more likely it is that the cost per unit will eventually fall.

Essilor, the lens-makers, have trained 2,500 of its Eye Mitra entrepreneurs to distribute these glasses, and a few million pairs have gone to users, reducing cost and eliminating the need for expensive lab infrastructure.

This is a great example of a design solution that could potentially have an impact on local manufacture. Local entrepreneurs could buy a fairly limited number of pre-cut lenses (let's say 100 Contour lenses for every 2,500 conventional lenses) and frames in a variety of styles, store them locally and then create an assembly-line business to fulfil orders from local testers.

As David Chute told us: 'For many reasons, it does not solve the entire problem, but it is a big step forward.'

Local manufacture would of course be boosted by 3D printing. Imagine if glasses could be produced cheaply by entrepreneurs within the countries whose populations are suffering from lack of vision care. Initially helped by their governments and NGOs, they would take on many of the roles currently performed by others today in the provision of spectacles.

Imagine the impact that would have on the lengthy, complicated and expensively marked-up supply chains that often stand in the way of easy distribution of glasses. Imagine the impact on the people themselves if they could choose the design of cheap spectacles and have them fitted by the very people who had just made them.

Pioneers in this field say it will eventually massively shorten the supply chain and crash the cost.

3D printing in the prototype stage has been with us for decades now. In more recent times, desktop-sized printers have helped many a start-up entrepreneur in their own specialised field.

For the uninitiated, like myself, I should first provide a brief explanation of 3D printing, and for that I am grateful to the *Independent* newspaper.[30]

'3D printers are a new generation of machines that can make everyday things. They're remarkable because they can produce different kinds of objects, in different materials, all from the same machine,' as Andrew Walker explained.

'A 3D printer can make pretty much anything from ceramic cups to plastic toys, metal machine parts, stoneware vases, fancy chocolate cakes or even (one day soon) human body parts.'

Andrew explained:

If you look closely at a page of text from your home printer, you'll see the letters don't just stain the paper, they're actually sitting slightly on top of the surface of the page.

In theory, if you printed over that same page a few thousand times, eventually the ink would build up enough layers on top of each other to create a solid 3D model of each letter. That idea of building a physical form out of tiny layers is how the first 3D printers worked.

You start by designing a 3D object on an ordinary home PC, connect it to a 3D printer, press 'print' and then sit back and watch. The process is a bit like making a loaf of sliced bread, but in reverse. Imagine baking each individual slice of bread and then gluing them together into a whole loaf (as opposed to making a whole loaf and then slicing it, like a baker does). That's basically what a 3D printer does.

The 3D printing process turns a whole object into thousands of tiny little slices, then makes it from the bottom-up, slice by slice. Those tiny layers stick together to form a solid object. Each layer can be very complex, meaning 3D printers can create moving parts like hinges and wheels as part of the same object. You could print a whole bike – handlebars, saddle, frame, wheels, brakes, pedals and chain – ready assembled, without using any tools. It's just a question of leaving gaps in the right places.

Thank you, Andrew!

As Euromonitor International reported, 3D printed technologies are already being adopted in the eyewear industry but particularly among spectacle frame and sunglass manufacturers.[31] Manufacturers are incorporating 3D printing to differentiate their products from those of their rivals.

Designer customised printed eyewear was available as early as 2012, when 3D printed eyewear first appeared in the eyewear industry. Mykita and ic! Berlin are examples of early movers who adopted 3D printing to manufacture frames.

At present, it appears, 3D printing is more expensive than traditional manufacturing production. However, these are early days and we must explore how the processes could help the mass market.

One challenge has been that while the technology can produce the frames, making lenses by 3D methods has proved altogether more difficult. However, it appears that we are on the verge of something big happening here.

We have spoken to the 3D printing optics company Luxexcel, which is based in Turnhout, Belgium and the first in the world to develop a unique technology to 3D print ophthalmic quality lenses.

The company has recently announced that its lenses have been independently tested and confirmed to be compliant with international standards. It launched its 3D printing technology for ophthalmic lenses at Vision Expo East in New York in April 2017, where it caused a massive wave of interest.

That is not surprising, because 3D glasses printing could one day have a huge impact on the ophthalmic market.

Marco de Visser, Luxexcel's business development manager, told us how the technology enabled very small droplets of liquid to merge together, forming a lens compliant with industry standards and compatible with other laboratory processes like tinting, coating and edging.

Marco said that Luxexcel would deliver the technology to selected American and European lens laboratories in the autumn of 2017 and the initial uses would centre on specialist lenses including prisms and high prescriptions.

Lens design is controlled by a tablet app, which will initially be provided to selected ophthalmic laboratories, and four unique lenses can be constructed concurrently over a period of one hour.

The key point that the company appears to have overcome is that its technology enables the manufacturing of lenses without the need for polishing.

Marco said Luxexcel can print lenses smooth from the printer with no need for processing afterwards, such as polishing. Using droplets rather than layers, as in normal 3D processes, leaves the final surface as smooth as the lens in any glasses.

Marco said:

We are carefully choosing our independent laboratory partners. We are taking this one step at a time. So at the moment, one machine makes four lenses per hour and we are in the early days.

They used to say it took fifty years for an analogue invention to reach full maturity and market use. But it will be much, much quicker here because it is digital, and look at how swiftly digital technologies are moving us forward. We are in an age of change.

He added that the invention would obviously aid our mission to bring sight testing and glasses to the developing world.

'There is already quite a bit of interest from developing countries,' he said. 'It could transform things there. Imagine if businesses within those countries were able to 3D print glasses internally. It would eliminate the cost of importation and mean there were far fewer stages in the supply chain.'

The process might also help to increase demand for the glasses in those countries if people knew they were being made locally and they could have a say in their design. If you broke your glasses, you could always go back to the shop and ask for another pair.

'We are confident the Luxexcel in-lab solution will have a huge impact on the eyewear world. You only had to see the interest we attracted during Vision Expo East New York to know that that is the case,' Marco said.

So this is exciting, and I know it may be some years ahead, but the visionaries like Kovin Naidoo are all for the eye-care world keeping a close watch on developments and looking for the opportunities it brings.

All are agreed that cultural barriers have to be broken down. But think how that might be helped if the future wearer was able to have a do-it-yourself say in the kind of glasses they are getting.

In the 3D world, when you break something and find it is out of production, you just hit print on your computer and build another one. As Andrew Walker said, it's a world that doesn't need lorries to deliver goods or warehouses to store them in, where nothing is ever out of stock and where there is less waste, packaging and pollution.

That sounds like a world that will help those of us trying to get glasses to all.

It's also a world where everyday items are made to meas-ure, to your requirements. That means furniture made to fit your home, shoes made to fit your feet, door handles made to fit your hand, meals printed to your tastes at the touch of a button. Even medicines, bones, organs and skin made to treat your injuries. And certainly, if I may add, glasses to fit your face and eyes.

As Andrew reported, like all new technologies, the industry hype is a few years ahead of the consumer reality. 3D is an emerging technology, which means, like home computers or mobile phones, most people will remain sceptical about needing one until everyone has got one... and then we'll all wonder how we ever managed without them.

So let's use the world of 3D to help us on our way. And in the meantime, let's make those prescription glasses available more cheaply – by reducing the import duties and taxes, and encouraging more local production.

CHAPTER 16

DEMAND: THE LAST TABOO

There have been two ages in the way children in the West regard glasses – Before Harry Potter and After Harry Potter.

J. K. Rowling's young wizard changed children's attitudes to wearing spectacles and reading. The idea that glasses were uncool was turned on its head in hours when children saw those movies.

He became their role model, and what their hero was wearing was cool with them.

In an interview with BBC *Newsround* in 2005, Rowling was asked why she gave Harry glasses. She replied:

> Because I had glasses all through my childhood and I was sick and tired of the person in the books who wore glasses was always the brainy one and it really irritated me and I wanted to read about a hero wearing glasses. It also has a symbolic function. Harry is the eyes on to the books in the sense that it is always Harry's point of view, so there was also that, you know, facet of him wearing glasses.

Decades before Harry, a real-life celebrity changed attitudes. Beatle John Lennon wore National Health Service spectacles and they became an instant hit with his fans.

When talking to leaders in this field of eye-care provision in the developing world – people like Kovin Naidoo, Jordan Kassalow, David Chute and Brian Doolan – one problem that comes up time and again is the cultural barrier to wearing spectacles. And we should not be surprised about that: how many of us know of friends, perhaps ourselves, who take their glasses off because they feel it makes them look more attractive? I know of people who memorise their speeches rather than deliver them wearing glasses. How many boys or girls on a night out take their glasses off because they want to look nicer? They might stumble around the dance floor but they will feel better in themselves. Millions in the West wear contact lenses despite them being more expensive and uncomfortable than glasses, primarily because of vanity.

And in some parts of the developing world, the stigmas go deeper: women fearing they have less chance of getting a partner if they are wearing spectacles, teachers advising pupils to take their glasses off when they go outside to play.

If we are to help the world see, people must feel there is a value to them wearing glasses. But they must also feel they are not uncool. On our Rwanda field trip, we saw people who were prescribed reading glasses and then spurned the chance of getting them for the equivalent of $1.50.

Jordan told us in an earlier chapter of the sad tale of the Chocó Indian woman who was thought to be blind, given glasses that helped her see well but took them back the next day because she was being ridiculed in her community.

There is a big cultural barrier here, and we should use all the instruments we have at our disposal to break it down.

The example of Harry Potter shows it can be done.

Let's look for the Pixar, Disney and Bollywood role models who could help us. It needs to be sensitively done; we need to avoid the impression of condescending Westerners telling the poor what is good for them. But we must use the combined power of such modern mediums to break down the taboo and show them glasses are cool.

Let's look at some of the examples we might deploy. There are glasses-wearing role models for the young and old in the big Disney films.

John Darling, in *Peter Pan*, is young but mature, sophisticated, smart – and of course wears specs.

Doc, the leader of the Seven Dwarves in *Snow White*, is getting on in years and wise – and wears glasses.

Edna Mode, from *The Incredibles*, a fashion designer for superheroes, wears them. Mrs Incredible sports an eye mask.

Several of the world's top actresses and supermodels – Jennifer Aniston, Megan Fox and Emma Watson among them – are proud wearers of spectacles. Jacqueline Fernandez, Sri Lanka's top model and actress, is often pictured wearing her spectacles.

The list goes on. What about *Minions*, the second-highest grossing animated film of all time? The 'heroes', who evolve from single-cell organisms at the dawn of time, exist to serve a series of unsuccessful masters like Napoleon. They have one or two eyes but wear glasses over them.

Let's take Pixar. Carl Fredricksen, the balloon salesman star of the acclaimed animated film *Up*, is a wearer of glasses. Carl was seventy-eight. Could we use him as part of a campaign to persuade grandparents of the value of seeing their grandchildren properly?

There are signs that the inbuilt reluctance to wearing glasses unless it's absolutely necessary is being broken down – at least in the developed world. J. C. Hinsley, UK country manager of one of the fastest-growing eyewear brands, Bailey Nelson, certainly thinks so.

Bailey Nelson, a bespoke eyewear company based in Sydney, Australia, insists that its appeal lies in the beauty and affordability of its handmade glasses.

Hinsley says wearing glasses is becoming cooler.

People often ask us whether we have glasses like those worn by Johnny Depp or other popular celebrities. They may not actually need glasses, but we can easily put lenses without a prescription in the frames. They just want to wear them.

More and more people are beginning to see glasses as a fashion accessory, and this removes the age-old negative stigma about glasses. Of course, the price is everything, but the way that glasses are viewed globally is important.

Andy Holliday, director of fundraising and communications at Vision Aid Overseas, which operates in five countries including Zambia and Ethiopia, is all for using local and internationally known role models to promote the wearing of glasses. 'If it is true that half the population of Africa will have a smartphone in ten years or less, let's show people that it is fashionable and necessary to wear glasses when you need them.' He added that one of the problems was that in some remote areas, people felt there was a stigma in wearing glasses and quite often the only people wearing glasses would be village elders.

Tinie Tempah is an English rapper and songwriter, born Patrick Chukwuemeka Okogwu.

He is known all over the world and is one of the leading stars of today. I have it on reasonable authority that he is big in some of the developing countries.

He is rarely without a pair of box glasses or round-rimmed specs. But he does not need them. He buys them for effect, because of what they do for him in his act. He told the *Daily Telegraph* that he first bought them from Brick Lane in London at £5 a pair. People said they looked good on him, so he bought more expensive frames.[32]

Tinie was born in Plumstead, London, in 1988. He is the son of Igbo parents from Nigeria. His middle name means 'God has done more' in the Igbo language. I can think of no better role model to persuade the young of the developing countries that they should wear glasses than a man whose parents hail from the country in Africa that I know so well and who wears them himself because they are cool.

I do not know Tinie Tempah, but I intend to meet him and ask him to help me in this mission.

In wondering how to tackle this problem, there was good guidance for me in Rwanda. It is one of the countries where an amazing movement called Girl Effect has been operating now for six years.

It has created pioneering and innovative media brands in different countries in a crusade to stop people seeing girls as part of the world poverty problem and start viewing them as one of the means of attacking that problem.

In Rwanda, Girl Effect launched *Ni Nyampinga*, a magazine, radio and mobile brand featuring characters and real-life role models who convey strong messages on how girls can achieve their full potential by staying on at school, getting access to health services, and choosing when to marry and have children. It has challenged perceptions of the value of girls in society and the belief they have only two roles: daughter and wife. Most of the millions reached by the brand say it has boosted their self-worth and confidence.

The magazine highlights local Rwandan girls like Console, who became a football coach; Utamuriza, who built her own nursery school; Esther, who overcame a disability to teach girls about reproductive health; or Butera Isheja Sandrine, who became a DJ.

The stories inspire Rwanda's female population and the magazine is a wonderful idea.

There is a lesson for us here. Can we persuade role models such as footballers and rock stars, both male and female, to do YouTube clips wearing spectacles and advising people to have eye tests?

Can we do something along the lines of the famous Nike 'If you let me play...' ad of 1995, stressing the positives to come from playing sport? The ad featured children from different backgrounds explaining how playing sports made them feel healthier and happier.

What about doing an 'If you helped me see...' ad, stressing that good vision would help everyone's potential?

From the start, girls have been at the heart of the *Ni Nyampinga*-branded media platform. They even had a hand in naming the brand, taking a traditional Kinyarwandan word describing the rite of passage from girl to woman and giving it a positive meaning – 'the beautiful girl inside and out, the one who makes good decisions'. They are the brand's ambassadors, travelling to towns and villages delivering the magazine and talking to girls about its contents.

By challenging set perceptions and showcasing female role models, *Ni Nyampinga* offers new skills and advice that girls cannot get elsewhere about education, sexual health and violence. Focusing on girl-led creation has driven the brand's cultural resonance and impact: it has directly reached more than 1 million girls, helping to unlock their true potential.

It does not stop in Rwanda. Girl Effect runs different brands for different countries. For example, in Malawi, Girl

Effect's innovation is a culture brand, Zathu, that, unlike any other NGO activity in the country, unites girls and boys for the very first time.

The brand seeks to address the negative social norms in Malawian society that result in significantly disproportionate rates of HIV in women compared to men – an adolescent girl in Malawi is eight times more likely to have HIV than a boy the same age.

Now over half of Rwandan girls read or listen to *Ni Nyampinga*; nearly 80 per cent of the total population are aware of it, including a high level of awareness among men (84 per cent) and boys (79 per cent).

Can we in the eye-care world build on the example of Girl Effect and create the same sense of value around glasses, the realisation that when you can see properly life is so much better? Maybe we can persuade Girl Effect to use their media outlets to show girls how wearing glasses when they need them can positively benefit their lives and careers.

If we can dispel these taboos, I believe we should then try to create a movement for change – one in which people demand the right to be given the chance to see clearly. We should engage community leaders in the campaign and launch radio and magazine campaigns based on existing models to persuade people in the developing countries of the value to them of wearing glasses.

And we should build on the staging of eye camps in towns and villages. Give people plenty of warning that nurses and health workers armed with glasses and screening tools will be coming on a certain day and advertise it in a positive way.

I turned to the retail world for their thoughts on this subject. Rupert Ellwood, head of marketing at Waitrose, consulted his top team and concluded that creating a demand movement in the developing countries was essential.

He proposed working up a simple, robust unit that could be sent to remote parts of countries, which would cleverly give people the experience of being able to see properly. He suggested a kind of film and picture show, relevant to the region in which the people live and including vistas, animals, people, even their own loved ones, messages on mobile phones – images that resonate. People would then be given glasses of different strengths and be able to compare what they have been seeing all their lives with what they can now see through glasses that meet their needs.

Rupert told me that such events, if they could be organised, would give people a compelling reason to have the glasses rather than ignoring their problem or even not realising they had one.

It would also mean that at one stroke people would know the kind of glasses strength that suited them and their lives could be changed.

I like Rupert's idea because it gets to the heart of what I believe we need more than anything else: showing people the value of glasses. Jordan Kassalow told us it was better for poor people to pay a small sum for glasses than have them handed down to them for free; it made them more valuable to them personally.

And that must be the key. There are examples out there of campaigns which have obviously failed to convince some people that what is being handed to them should be used for the purpose intended.

Millions of insecticide-coated mosquito nets sent by global charities to protect people from the risk of malaria have been misused all over Africa by people employing them to catch fish, or for other purposes.[33]

Impoverished families have chosen to put the need to feed themselves ahead of the desire to prevent disease. But it has had the unforeseen impact of depleting fish stocks, because the nets, designed to keep the mozzies out, have caught the tiniest fish before they have anywhere near matured.

In this case, people might indeed have seen the value of the nets. But to them there was an even more valuable use to which they could be put. They had to feed their families.

It confirms to me that we have to work with the people, often through their community leaders, to help them with their own problems. Their first reaction might well be to reject help imposed on them without consultation. They must feel that they 'own' the solutions.

Others who work in this field of challenging cultural norms stress to me the importance of creating brands over products. A brand is easy for people to recognise, adopt, champion and share.

I was told by Natalie Au, director of gender at Girl Effect:

People can wrap their whole identity around brands. They are based on an 'idea' so they have multiple touch points – you don't just reach the customer right in front of you, but all those around him or her. The brand can exist and mean different things to different people. It can be expressed, shared and can multiply way beyond one shop, one advertising campaign, or one product. Brands can mobilise the power of media and technology.

You can reach people at scale with a brand. Better yet, the more established these brands are, the more influence they have and their value for money increases.

Brands like Jamie Oliver and Sesame Street create content that, while entertaining and therefore attractive to the masses, exposes people to storylines, new ways of thinking that educate and inform – healthy school meals, domestic abuse, autism and sexual health are all difficult topics that have been discussed and exposed on these programmes/through these brands – reaching millions of people in a completely unique way. What did 'brand Jamie Oliver' do for healthy school meals? It encouraged progress much faster than any traditional NGO or educational programme.

So we may have something to learn here. Can we find home-grown storylines, the ambassadors, role models and characters that truly resonate with the people we are trying to reach and give them a new perception of what it means to wear glasses? We have found many examples during the course of writing this book of people whose lives have been altered completely by the acquisition of glasses. Let's make sure we get those stories out there. Let's use the celebrities. Come on, Tinie Tempah – give us your support. Organisations like Girl Effect have shown the way. Let's follow.

CHAPTER 17

CONCLUSION: THE ANSWER IS GLASSES – SEE FOR YOURSELF

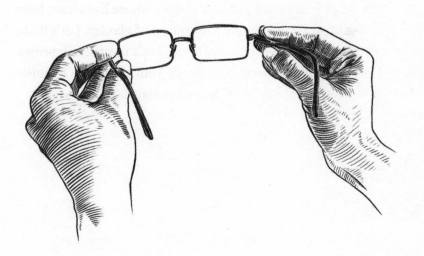

'All she needed was glasses,' said David Chute, one of the world's leading eye-care experts, at a gathering I organised for campaigners, inventors and practitioners in April 2017.

An elderly seamstress in Guatemala was a major source of income in her family. But her eyesight deteriorated so badly that she found it difficult to do her job. Her husband and daughter worked. Her granddaughter lived with her.

There was no alternative. The girl had to be taken out of school to help her grandmother thread the needles so that she could go on sewing and making garments to keep her grandchildren in food and clothes. This phenomenon is all too common in parts of the developing world.

But eventually the grandmother was given a simple eye test and found to need reading glasses. She was one of the 7 million recipients of glasses from the supplying organisation RestoringVision, of which David is a board member. Her granddaughter was able to return to school.

'All she needed was glasses.' That one sentence is the reason for the Clearly campaign and for this book.

In writing it, I hope I have succeeded in doing three things. First, explaining the pervasiveness of the issue of poor vision, which affects a third of the world's population and is holding back prosperity in developing countries. Second, documenting the inspiring progress that is taking place across the globe by inventors, practitioners, and – in some but not enough places – governments, too. Third, setting out a clear series of solutions to get glasses – a 700-year-old invention – on the noses of everyone who needs them.

The first optical revolution occurred because the reduced cost and greater opportunity to acquire information and knowledge became widespread as a result of the invention of the Gutenberg printing press. With the spread of smart-phones and the internet again reducing the cost and increasing the opportunity to acquire information and knowledge, I believe we are on the cusp of the second optical revolution, when the promise of glasses on the faces of everyone who needs them can finally be fulfilled within this generation.

But I don't want this book or these ideas to sit on the shelf collecting dust. The plates are shifting and now is the time for action. So I will conclude with a collective call to arms: to international organisations, to governments around the world, and to you – the believer. But let me start with my own commitment.

I was fortunate to be born into wealth and to have the opportunity to become what is sometimes termed a 'venture philanthropist'. This means that I am not a passive donor but a funder with a clear mission. Every day I am driven by the belief that if a human is to land on Mars by the 2030s, I want to ensure that the whole world can see it.

Over the past decade, I have given a personal commitment and will continue to do so. I am passionate about the power of innovation, which is why I invested in Adlens, a product that gives the wearer the ability to adjust to their own vision and simplifies distribution. It's also why I set up the Clearly Vision Prize to stimulate the best ideas to tackle poor vision from around the world.

But my experience of funding and leading Vision for a Nation in Rwanda – encouraging though that was – taught me that if we are to tackle this issue at the global level, we need a global campaign to keep the pressure on the international community and ensure that this issue can no longer be forgotten. So, in the years ahead, expect to hear from me and the Clearly campaign as we try to raise the profile of poor vision.

Our first target will be the international organisations. We need the world's leaders to embrace this issue and consider its impact. So many of them wear glasses that I hope they will listen. This should start with a discussion and new commitment at the Commonwealth summit in London in April 2018, which can be used as a springboard for further progress in other institutions.

In 1999, the World Health Organization agreed an ambitious goal of eliminating avoidable blindness by 2020. But in truth, relatively little progress has been made in achieving this and poor vision barely gets a look in. Indeed, the WHO does not even keep proper records on the number of people who need a pair of glasses. The opportunity is there for the WHO to raise its ambition, put the resources in place, and measure its progress.

My blueprint sets out the problem of import duties and taxes, and that of regulations which artificially add to the cost of getting a pair of glasses to someone who needs them. So, in keeping with their mandates, the World Trade Organization and World Bank have the chance to take a lead on this issue. In the past, these organisations faced criticism for calling for the removal of regulations or taxes which protected consumers or workers. But these rules are ripe for removal as they only protect a vested interest.

Next, we need the big multilateral donors – like the World Bank, the European Union and regional banks such as the African Development Bank and Asian Development Bank – to begin prioritising this issue. By providing upfront resources – for training and infrastructure – it is possible to pump-prime a domestic market for glasses, as Rwanda has shown. Innovative financing models – like payment-by-results – are another way of incentivising innovation and encouraging collaborative thinking from practitioners on the ground.

Bilateral donors can also build on the work they've already done. The Department for International Development in the UK has been a generous donor to Sightsavers and the Queen Elizabeth Diamond Jubilee Trust for their work on preventable blindness. Both they and the United States Agency for International Development gave funding for Vision for a Nation. The Australian Agency for International Development has funded the Fred Hollows Foundation. But these donors could help mobilise resouces within developing countries to put in place primary eye-care systems that are available to all – as has taken place in Rwanda.

But global and developed world action on its own is not enough. Developing countries themselves need to understand and embrace this issue. Universal healthcare is a major component of countries' delivery of the sustainable development goals, but we need them to be explicit about including primary eye care. Only clear demand from developing countries will unlock real funding.

And what about you? I hope as this book ends you feel as energised as I do and as motivated to do something about it. So let me suggest two courses of action.

First, if you wear contact lenses or glasses, try going a day – or even an hour – without wearing them. Obviously avoid operating any machinery or driving, but see how difficult it is to get up in the morning, to find your way to work or college, to take part in the normal course of your day, to come home in the evening and read your kids a bedtime story or make dinner or watch the evening news. If you don't need glasses, talk to your partner, a parent or a colleague who does and get them to describe it. Remember: that's how a third of the world lives.

Second, get involved in the Clearly campaign. Like any organisation trying to change the world, we are only as powerful as the size of our support. You can make a difference. We have launched a petition calling on world leaders to wake up to the issue of poor vision. Add your name at www. clearly.world/action and send a message to let them know that now is the time to act, then join the conversation online using #eyeswideopen.

·O·O·

The race to Mars is on. When a human finally lands on the red planet, everyone must be able to see it. There should be no excuses.

The battle has been joined. We know the answers are there. We just need the will to do it. So I say to politicians and global authorities – show us and the billions lacking access to clear vision that you understand this problem and will help all of us to do something about it.

The answer, as the elderly woman from Guatemala found, is on the end of our noses.

ABOUT THE AUTHOR

I was born in Hong Kong on 19 July 1961. My father and his father were born in mainland China. My grandfather had a humble upbringing but became a highly successful businessman, launching an enamelware business in Shanghai. In 1947, anticipating the Communist Revolution in China, he moved the family and business to Hong Kong, then under British rule. He then set up a business in Indonesia and moved from there to Africa, eventually consolidating the business in Nigeria, setting up another enamelware and consumer products company there.

My earliest childhood memory was the Swissair flight via Bangkok, Bombay (as Mumbai was known then), Athens and Zurich on the way to Lagos, Nigeria. It was such an exciting adventure, like camping, as, even in economy-class travel in those days, I could sleep on the floor of the plane in front of our seats.

In Nigeria, we lived a frills-free but comfortable expatriate life in a house across the street from our factory, which was opened the year I was born. As our house was so close to the factory, our dining room doubled as the canteen for senior staff at lunch and often for dinner. Senior staff and business associates would join us, so much of our mealtime conversation revolved around business.

I found those adult conversations interesting and would patiently listen and learn. One story which is part of our family folklore was relayed by the factory production manager. He said that I rang him one day and told him that too much smoke was coming out of the furnace chimney, wasting fuel. He lamented that his fate in life was clear – to be at the service of not only two but three generations of the Chen family, Grandpa ZaoMing, father Robert and young James. Looking back, it certainly showed my interest from an early age in business, but I wonder whether my concern about too much smoke from the chimney was also an early indication of interest in social activism.

I now remember how few Africans were wearing glasses, whereas many expatriates from richer countries were. That memory has regularly come back to me since we launched Clearly.

We returned to Hong Kong every other year and, at the insistence of my mother, would take the opportunity on our way back to see different European cities. I recall occasionally being impatient at visiting countless cathedrals, tombs and museums, but I loved the contrast of Europe with Africa, the orderliness versus the chaos, the cool and dry versus the hot and humid. The differences were striking and exhilarating. I remember seeing snow for the first time in Zurich and opening my mouth to catch all the falling flakes.

I was in an unusual position. My family hailed from a developing-world country and had a business halfway across the world in another developing country. But I saw plenty of the developed world in my youth. It meant that in my formative years I could experience and compare at first hand economic and cultural diversity and develop an identity that was not rooted in one culture or set of norms. I was lucky.

I would call myself a global citizen. I would feel unease and discomfort at being identified as part of the 'establishment' of any society.

Seeing on television at the age of eleven the Phoenician Hotel in Beirut going up in flames, the same hotel where I had stayed less than three years earlier, and recalling our happy holiday there with a Lebanese family who were business associates and friends of my family in Nigeria, left a lasting impression on me of how you must never expect things to stay as they are for long.

At the age of ten, I was enrolled in a Jesuit boarding school in the Lancashire countryside in England. It was a complete shock to my system. It was a challenge to adapt, but the in-built adversity of boarding school life helped me to develop a resilience which has proved advantageous in later life.

When I was thirteen, my parents emigrated to America in order to obtain residency and citizenship. By now they were stateless refugees from the Communist Revolution in China and they were concerned by the implications of the return of Hong Kong to China in 1997. I joined them in upstate New York, where my uncle was an employee of the New York City water works. I enrolled in the local high school and then went on to the University of Chicago.

The university was academically demanding. I was far from being a top student, but the liberal arts curriculum was terrific and I am grateful for the intellectual grounding that helped me make sense of an increasingly complicated world.

After graduation, I worked for the Prudential insurance company in investment accounting and quickly discovered that I had neither the interest, the temperament nor the capacity for the work. I started at Columbia Business School while helping with my family's investments in real estate in New York. I found business school to be dreary and dry and made the decision to quit and start a restaurant called Good Enough to Eat. I fell out with my father, who wrote into his will that I would be disinherited if I did not complete my business degree.

I would contend that my restaurant was a critical success, but it was a financial failure. I admit it. Despite my best efforts and belief in the restaurant, we had insurmountable problems. Having to cope with failure, especially on a project in which I had invested such high hopes, was a bitter but important life experience that has served me well later in life.

Fortunately for me, the work I had done for the family's US real estate holdings helped me to land a job as Asia Pacific representative of Trammell Crow International, a large family-held real estate concern. The Trammell Crow enterprise was organised as a family office and it prompted me to propose to my family setting up such an office for our enterprises. After much resistance, my father relented after I pledged to pay for the establishment of the family office out of my own savings. And so the family firm Legacy Advisors was launched in late 1994 – it still runs our affairs.

The Asian financial crisis clearly demonstrated the advantages of utilising the family office concept of risk management and diversification to achieve superior investment results and at the end of a quarterly family meeting in 1998, my father took me aside and gave me a cheque repaying me for the cost of setting up the family office. He said to me, 'I get it now.'

The rift was over. My relationship with my father changed in a very meaningful way. We became very close and we were able to develop a trusting, respectful, supportive and loving relationship.

It was also at this time that he shared with me his struggles with his philanthropic engagement with our ancestral hometown, Qidong, in Jiangsu province across the Yangtze River from Shanghai, where he had done so much. In China at this time, charitable giving was common among the wealthy diaspora but my father's personal and deep engagement rather than simple cheque-writing resulted in much better outcomes than the experiences of many of his peers. By the late 1990s, he was feeling it was time to call it a day but I felt that his legacy of philanthropic engagement over the previous fifteen years was inspiring and worth continuing, although in a different, more structured way.

To do this, I convinced him to set up a family foundation. The Chen Yet-Sen Family Foundation articles of association were the final documents my dad signed before he died. The work our philanthropic arm has done in the past fourteen years is very much inspired by his example of not just donating money but understanding the real needs of the community we are trying to serve and spending time and effort to meet that need. I also serve as the non-executive chairman of Wahum Group Holdings, the holding company of our Nigeria-based business.

In this latest phase of our work at the family foundation, we have devoted our time and effort to enhancing early childhood literacy and developing the reading culture in the communities we serve. We strive to be the go-to resource in this territory and to develop ever greater domain expertise in it. The conceptual model with vision correction follows a similar path of patient engagement and accumulation of domain expertise through experimentation, not simply financial assistance.

My journey started with a chance encounter in 2004 with Professor Josh Silver, a former physics professor at the University of Oxford and the man who first saw the full potential of the modern fluid-filled adjustable lens. I had been told about Josh's invention by a business broker. I was curious to learn more and googled Josh's name and found his Oxford email address. He invited me to tea at the Commonwealth Club in London and our partnership was under way.

My own experience meant I could personally empathise with the issue of poor vision and its impact. However, beyond this empathy and a significant portion of my life spent in Africa and Asia, I had no understanding about anything to do with vision or optics, nor the issue of access to vision correction.

I immediately grasped the potential of adjustable power lenses to have an impact on vision correction in the developing world, where distribution and logistics are fragile and expensive. I saw that the wide range of the lenses could simplify an extremely complex and costly deployment of glasses. You may find this hard to believe, but it's true. One pair of adjustable glasses can cover the same combination of lens powers as 2,400 separate pairs of prescription glasses. What equally intrigued me was the possibility that this technology could also be applicable to the developed world market for glasses. At the time, in the early 2000s, the concept of the social enterprise was particularly in vogue, although few feasible models existed. I thought this fluid-filled adjustable-power lens technology could be an exemplary example of an achievable 'social enterprise'.

Adjustable lenses closely model the eye's natural dynamic behaviour, restoring vision quality and control. Each lens can be manually adjusted to an individual's near, intermediate or distance vision requirement.

The real power of adjustable eyeglasses is that anyone with poor vision can use them and within seconds get an instant life-changing 'wow' effect as the blurry world transforms into a clear one. It is instant, it doesn't require complicated explanations of how the eye works, and the person needn't wait a week to get their glasses.

When J and J Technologies was formed, later to be renamed Adlens, Josh and I set out to develop further the technology, with the aim of producing viable products that could be sold in the developed markets commercially as well as utilised in the developing world for vision correction. It seemed revolutionary then, almost naïve now. We hired Julian Lambert, a seasoned professional on secondment from the UK Department for International Development, to begin a dialogue with the development and aid community on raising awareness of the adjustable glasses to find development partners and sources of funding.

Julian focused his effort on lobbying the World Bank, but after more than two years of effort and a significant number of pilot engagements with various NGOs, it became clear that the bank would be unlikely to step up as a major funder and the NGOs seemed less than enthusiastic. At this point, the social enterprise concept was ditched. Adlens then became a commercial venture with a social purpose and I decided to set up a charity – VFAN. I am pleased that Adlens remains involved in so far as it has donated glasses or sold at cost to the charity and seconded staff members with technical expertise as needed by VFAN.

Throughout this book, I have insisted that if a human is to be put on Mars in the next two decades, the whole world must be able to see it.

And now I have a bit of news for readers. Both NASA, the American Space Agency, and the European Space Agency have shown an interest in using the fluid-filled adjustable glasses developed by my Adlens company for their astronauts in future missions. We are in touch.

It would indeed be wonderful if glasses similar to those we used to pioneer our Rwanda efforts, and now distributed in many other countries, went to Mars. Elon Musk hopes that one day the planet can be colonised through the partnership between NASA and his company, SpaceX.

Glasses that adjust the power of lenses to suit the user's needs are essential for lengthy space missions. Prolonged exposure to micro-gravity during space travel causes vision to fluctuate in unpredictable ways. The fixed-lens technology that most use today will not be suitable for those who take up the challenge to settle on Mars. Our space travellers will need to adjust as they go if they are to see what they are doing.

And, as I wrote to Elon in an email, while innovations of this sort might well be used by those who travel to distant planets, they can be used today to disrupt the status quo and slash the cost of glasses for the billions who need them. The race to Mars has started. Let's get glasses to all the people who need them here on earth first.

REFERENCES

Chapter 1: Wake Up World

1   We use this figure throughout the book to describe the number of people worldwide who are affected by poor vision and need a pair of glasses but cannot get access to any. The figure derives from a methodology developed by the Boston Consulting Group for Essilor and widely cited, including by the World Economic Forum: Smith, E., Chen, W., Congdon, N., Frick, K., Kassalow, J., Naidoo, K., Sloan, J. A. (2016). 'Eyeglasses for Global Development: Bridging the Visual Divide'.

2   Gordois, A., Cutler, H., Pezzullo, L., Gordon, K., Cruess, A., Winyard, S., Hamilton, W., Chua, K. (2012). 'An estimation of the worldwide economic and health burden of visual impairment'. *Global Public Health*, 7 (5), 465–81.

3   *The Atlantic*, 'The 50 Greatest Breakthroughs Since the Wheel'. https://www.theatlantic.com/magazine/archive/2013/11/innovations-list/309536/

4   Fricke, T. R., Holden, B. A., Wilson, D. A., Schlenther, G., Naidoo, K. S., Resnikoff, S., Frick, K. D. (2012). 'Global cost of correcting vision impairment from uncorrected refractive error'. *Bulletin of the World Health Organization*, 90 (10), 728–38.

5   Armstrong, K. L., Jovic, M., Vo-Phuoc, J. L., Thorpe, J. G., Doolan, B. L. (2012). 'The global cost of eliminating avoidable blindness'. *Indian Journal of Ophthalmology*, 60 (5), 475–80.

6   a) Fred Hollows Foundation. http://www.hollows.org/getattachment/au/Annual-Report-2015/2015-FHF-Group-Financial-Statements-v20160330-FINAL-Signed.pdf.aspx
    b) SightSavers International. http://www.sightsavers.org/wp-content/uploads/2016/09/2015_AnnualReport_Accessible_WEB.pdf
    c) Orbis International. http://gbr.orbis.org/page/-/Orbis%20final%202015%20Audit%2012-31-15.pdf
    d) CBM. http://www.cbmuk.org.uk/wp-content/uploads/2016/04/MU21187-CBM-Annual-Report-accessible.pdf
    e) Brien Holden Vision Institute. http://develop.brienholdenvision.org/bhvi_2015/images/pdfs/resources/annual_reviews/foundation/11-12_bhvi_report.pdf
    f) Lions International. https://www.lionsclubs.org/resources/all/pdfs/lcif/lcif30_14-15.pdf

g) Light for the World. https://www.light-for-the-world.org/sites/lfdw_org/files/download_files/lftw_ar_2014_15_screen_0.pdf

h) Optometry Giving Sight. http://www.givingsight.org/images/media_centre/AnnualReport_2015_V9_acr.pdf

i) Helen Keller International. http://www.hki.org/sites/default/files/attach/2016/07/HKI_Annual_Report_2015_Finalweb.pdf

j) *Financial Times*: 'Luxottica and Essilor agree Euro 50bn merger'. https://www.ft.com/content/a4b43936-db78-11e6-9d7c-be108f1c1dce

Chapter 3: The Four Ds: Obstacles to Progress

7   Smith, E., Chen, W., Congdon, N., Frick, K., Kassalow, J., Naidoo, K., Sloan, J. A. (2016). 'Eyeglasses for Global Development: Bridging the Visual Divide'. World Economic Forum.

8   Kapoor, A., Goyal, S. (2015) 'VisionSpring in India: Enabling Affordable Eyeglasses for the Poor'. HBS W14767, Management Development Institute Gurgaon and Richard Ivey School of Business Foundation.

9   Coppola, E. (2012). 'The Eyewear Market: Luxottica's Leadership, Strategy and Acquisitions'. Libera Università Internazionale degli Studi Sociali Guido Carli, Rome.

10   'International Optical Trade Analysis: Frames June 2016'. The Vision Council, Virginia.

11   'International Optical Trade Analysis: Lenses June 2016'. The Vision Council, Virginia.

12   'Vision Care Market Quarterly Overview: December 2016'. The Vision Council, Virginia.

Chapter 4: Counting the Cost

13   Gordois, A., Cutler, H., Pezzullo, L., Gordon, K. (2012). 'An estimation of the worldwide economic and health burden of visual impairment'. *Global Public Health.* 7 (5), 465–81.

14   World Health Organization: 'Spending on Health: A Global Overview'. http://www.who.int/mediacentre/factsheets/fs319/en/

15   Dieleman, J., Murray, C. J. L., Haakenstad, A. (2016). 'Financing Global Health 2015: Development assistance steady on the path to new Global Goals'. Institute for Health Metrics and Evaluation.

16   Smith, E., Chen, W., Congdon, N., Frick, K., Kassalow, J., Naidoo, K., Sloan, J. A. (2016). 'Eyeglasses for Global Development: Bridging the Visual Divide'. World Economic Forum.

17   Ma, X., Zhou, Z., Yi, H., Pang, X., Shi, Y., Chen, Q., Meltzer, M. E., le Cessie,
      S., He, M., Rozelle, S., Liu, Y., Congdon, N. (2014). 'Effect of providing free
      glasses on children's educational outcomes in China: cluster randomized con-
      trolled trial'. *British Medical Journal.* 349, g5740.
18   Fred Hollows Foundation (2013): 'Investing in Vision: The costs and benefits
      of ending avoidable blindness'. Pricewaterhouse Coopers, Australia.
19   Boston Consulting Group and Essilor (2012): 'The Social and Economic
      Impact of Poor Vision'. https://vii-production.s3.amazonaws.com/uploads/
      research_article/pdf/51356f5ddd57fa3f6b000001/VisionImpactInsti-
      tute-WhitePaper-Nov12.pdf

Chapter 6: The Mystery of the Human Eye

20   Yong, E. (February 2016). 'Inside the Eye: Nature's most exquisite crea-
      tion'. *National Geographic.* http://www.nationalgeographic.com/magazine/
      2016/02/evolution-of-eyes/
21   Xiang, F., He, M., Morgan, I. G. (2012). 'The impact of parental myopia on
      myopia in Chinese children: population-based evidence'. *Optometry and
      Vision Science.* 89 (10), 1487–96.

Chapter 7: The Great Glasses Rush

22   Johnson, Steven. (2014). *How We Got to Now: Six Innovations that Made the
      Modern World.* Penguin.
23   Zeiss. (2012). 'The History of Spectacles'. https://www.zeiss.co.uk/vision-
      care/en_gb/better-vision/understanding-vision/lenses-and-solutions/
      the-history-of-spectacles.html

Chapter 8: Giants of the Eye World

24   Lewallen, S., Etya'ale, D., Bedri Kello, A., Courtright, P. (November 2012).
      'Non-physician cataract surgeons in Sub-Saharan Africa: situation analysis'.
      Tropical Medicine and International Health, 17.

Chapter 9: The Inventors

25   http://reap.fsi.stanford.edu/
26   http://www.smartfocusvision.com/about.html

Chapter 10: A Vision for Rwanda

27   Amnesty International Report 2014/15 – Rwanda, 25 February 2015. http://www.refworld.org/docid/54f07da57.html

28   UN Development Index Report. http://hdr.undp.org/en/countries/profiles/RWA

Chapter 11: On the Edge of Change

29   Graham, M. (5 April 2016). 'Opternative fighting states that try to ban its online eye exams'. *Chicago Tribune.* http://www.chicagotribune.com/bluesky/originals/ct-opternative-legislation-online-exams-bsi-20160405-story.html

Chapter 15: Dollars: Cost Down, Local Production Up

30   Walker, A. (21 June 2013). '3D printing for dummies: how do 3D printers work?' http://www.independent.co.uk/life-style/gadgets-and-tech/features/3d-printing-for-dummies-how-do-3d-printers-work-8668937.html

31   http://blog.euromonitor.com/2016/05/eyewear-3d-printing.html

Chapter 16: Demand: The Last Taboo

32   Garratt, S., (25 March 2014). 'Tinie Tempah: the most stylish man in music'. *Daily Telegraph.* http://www.telegraph.co.uk/men/fashion-and-style/10711786/Tinie-Tempah-the-most-stylish-man-in-music.html

33   Gettleman, J. (24 January 2015). 'Meant to Keep Malaria Out, Mosquito Nets Are Used to Haul Fish In'. *New York Times.* https://www.nytimes.com/2015/01/25/world/africa/mosquito-nets-for-malaria-spawn-new-epidemic-overfis

INDEX